MAMIE
DOUD
EISENHOWER

MODERN FIRST LADIES

Lewis L. Gould, Editor

MAMIE DOUD EISENHOWER

THE GENERAL'S FIRST LADY

MARILYN IRVIN HOLT

UNIVERSITY PRESS OF KANSAS

© 2007 by the University Press of Kansas

All rights reserved

Published by the University Press of Kansas (Lawrence, Kansas 66045),
which was organized by the Kansas Board of Regents and is operated
and funded by Emporia State University, Fort Hays State University,
Kansas State University, Pittsburg State University, the University
of Kansas, and Wichita State University

Library of Congress Cataloging-in-Publication Data

Holt, Marilyn Irvin, 1949-

Mamie Doud Eisenhower : the general's first lady / Marilyn Irvin Holt.

p. cm.—(Modern first ladies)

Includes bibliographical references and index.

ISBN 978-0-7006-1539-1 (cloth : alk. paper)

1. Eisenhower, Mamie Doud, 1896–1979.

2. President's spouses—United States—Biography.

3. Generals' spouses—United States—Biography.

I. Title.

E837.E4H65 2007

973.921092—dc22

[B]

2007017871

British Library Cataloguing-in-Publication Data is available.

Printed in the United States of America

10 9 8 7 6 5 4 3 2 1

The paper used in this publication meets the minimum requirements of the
American National Standard for Permanence of Paper for Printed Library
Materials Z39.48–1992.

To Daniel

CONTENTS

EDITOR'S FOREWORD

In the past twenty-five years, the historical reputation of President Dwight D. Eisenhower has rebounded. This process of revisionism has not, however, produced the same upward reappraisal for his wife, Mamie Doud Eisenhower. Her contributions as first lady from 1953 to 1961 have faded from memory. Beside the glamour and beauty of her successor, Jacqueline Kennedy, Mrs. Eisenhower has seemed, with her trademark bangs and her wifely devotion to her husband, an archaic personality from the bygone days of the staid 1950s.

As Marilyn Irvin Holt shows in this sensitive and perceptive study of Mamie Eisenhower in the White House, there was far more to this neglected first lady than the clichés that have surrounded her. Mamie Eisenhower matured in the demanding world of the wife of a soldier, and she brought that ethos to the White House in 1953. Popular during her husband's presidency, Mrs. Eisenhower worked hard on the social side of the White House with an emphasis on cultural events and charitable causes that Holt skillfully brings out. The sense that there was a great shift in tone and style from the Eisenhower to the Kennedy presidency may need some revision in light of Holt's work.

Most of all, Holt recaptures Mamie Eisenhower's winning personality that made her such an important element both in the success of her husband and in the cultural milieu of the 1950s. While remaining a discreet figure as Dwight Eisenhower achieved world fame, his wife did much in her own subtle ways to sustain him and to expand his intrinsic appeal to the American people. Holt's engaging narrative should stimulate a reconsideration of a first lady who put her own stamp on the institution based on the lessons she had learned during decades in the tightly knit culture of the U.S. Army. Mamie Eisenhower too had a hidden-hand style that makes her worthy of the fascinating study that Marilyn Holt has provided for the Modern First Ladies series.

Lewis L. Gould

PREFACE

The Modern First Ladies series published by the University Press of Kansas was designed to examine the institution of first lady as it has been shaped and defined by the women who have held that position during the twentieth century. Mamie Doud Eisenhower, the last first lady to be born in the nineteenth century, came to the White House in the 1950s. Her personal style of open friendliness and devotion to her friends and family were a good match for the family-centered, baby boom fifties, but to understand Mamie Eisenhower's approach to the role of first lady it is necessary to first consider her life as an army officer's wife. To ignore those experiences, as well as the military culture as she knew it, diminishes the context of Mrs. Eisenhower's life as first lady.

People outside the military have little understanding of what that life entails or realize that there is a tradition of conduct that is expected not only of those who serve but also of their spouses. The traditions and expectations for military spouses developed out of the military frontier of the nineteenth century when women followed their army husbands to post assignments that were oftentimes at the edge of American expansion and control. The women developed networks for moral support and social contact, while at the same time transporting their cultural values and sense of Victorian domesticity to the life of the post.

At the time Mamie became the wife of a junior officer in 1916, she could expect many of the same sort of experiences encountered by her nineteenth-century counterparts. There was the probability of numerous moves, the possibility of living in substandard housing, and the challenge of running a household on her husband's often insufficient army pay. She also learned that the deference to rank demanded among enlisted personnel and officers created class distinctions among wives. Women relied on one another, but the wives of senior officers had the unspoken task of being leaders, much as their husbands looked after the men in their charge. In this rank-conscious environment, a husband's rank gave his wife her status. When the husband advanced, so did she. Women saw their husbands' careers as their careers. Most accepted the premise that they could hurt their husbands' chances at promotion if they failed to volunteer for worthwhile projects such as working for the Red Cross or if they failed to fulfill social obligations.

These expectations for women living within the military culture influenced Mamie Eisenhower's conduct as a military wife and her heartfelt conviction that she shared in her husband's career. In effect, Mamie Eisenhower's years as an army wife laid the foundation for her approach to the role as first lady. Her husband's rise to Supreme Allied Commander in Europe during World War II and then his unprecedented position as head of Supreme Headquarters, Allied Powers Europe, in 1951–1952, placed her in situations that were distinctly different from those of other first ladies. By the time Mamie Eisenhower came to the White House, she had lived overseas during three separate periods of her life; she already knew what it was like to be an object of media interest; and she had not only met, but been on familiar terms with, numerous heads of foreign governments.

This volume was organized to include a study of Mrs. Eisenhower during the years between World War I and World War II when, as an army wife, her husband's postings included Paris, Panama, the Philippines, and numerous military bases within the United States. Also of relevance are her experiences during World War II and the immediate postwar period when, after a brief time at Columbia University, General Eisenhower returned to Europe. These varied situations influenced Mamie Eisenhower and her approach to defining and fulfilling the role of first lady.

It was also important to place Mrs. Eisenhower within the context of the 1950s. "Mamie Pink" and "Mamie Bangs" were part of that decade's popular culture. Her repeated references to herself as a "housewife" harmonized with the era's image of domesticity. Young couples beginning families of their own and older couples looking forward to grandchildren could relate to Mamie's devotion to her husband, son, and grandchildren. Mamie's personal style, fashion sense, and desire to bring sparkle to the White House also resonated with Americans who were quite willing, after years of economic depression and wartime shortages, to participate in a growing consumer economy that promised material comforts. Without artifice, Mamie Eisenhower was able to project the image of being the friend next door, a woman who shared the expectations of thousands of Americans for the promise of the American Dream. Mamie reflected back to the public its own desire for "normal" times.

That is not to suggest, of course, that the 1950s were an idyllic period in American history. Nostalgia for the era, which some have naively defined as a simpler time, has overshadowed the decade's very real political and social conflicts, including the fear of communism, the threat of nuclear attack, and the beginnings of the modern civil rights movement in the United States. Mamie was quite aware of the large, and often dangerous, problems that faced the country domestically and internationally, but she did not confront these issues by speaking directly before the American public or trying to influence administration policy behind the scenes. She held to the position that the American people had elected her husband, not her. Her role, as she saw it, was to be a nonpolitical first lady, standing as a representative for the American people.

The foundation for this volume's research was Mamie Doud Eisenhower's Papers at the Eisenhower Presidential Library in Abilene, Kansas. They are divided into a series of collections that correspond to the chapters in her life. There is the prepresidential collection; the Columbia University Series; the SHAPE Series; the White House Series, which alone totals more than 40,000 pages; and two series for Mrs. Eisenhower's postpresidential years. In addition, the library holds videos of interviews with the first lady; videos of interviews with Eisenhower family members; and the museum, which has a gallery devoted to the first lady, holds an impressive collection of Mamie Eisenhower's personal possessions.

For their great, and substantial, assistance I would like to thank the knowledgeable and talented library staff. In particular, there is archivist Tom Branigar, who processed much of the Mamie Doud Eisenhower document collection and who is an expert on both the Eisenhower and the Doud genealogy. I also wish to acknowledge Dennis Medina, museum curator, for his insights and extensive knowledge. He had the unique experience of knowing Mrs. Eisenhower and working with her in collecting, identifying, and exhibiting her personal items. And a special thanks to Kathy Struss for her help in finding video and still photographs for this publication. My gratitude also extends to Steven Benedict and Douglas Price, who shared their memories of the 1952 presidential campaign; Irwin Gellman, who read portions of the manuscript and offered good advice; and members of the Eisenhower family, who responded to my queries with kind patience.

MAMIE
DOUD
EISENHOWER

CHAPTER 1

THE MILITARY LIFE

Not long before her death in 1979, Mamie Doud Eisenhower was interviewed by Barbara Walters at the Eisenhower Gettysburg farm. As the interview came to a close, Walters asked how the former first lady wanted to be remembered. Clearly surprised, Mrs. Eisenhower paused. "I hadn't even thought about such a thing," she answered. After a minute, she added, "Just as a good friend." The response said a great deal about Mamie Eisenhower. She genuinely liked people, took an interest in them, and was quick to offer advice, a compliment, or an observation. As first lady, she responded to thousands of letters from the general public, and she greeted untold numbers on the campaign trail and in the White House. She placed great value on close relationships with longtime friends and her family. "[She was] probably the best friend anybody could have," said grandson David.[1]

Mamie Doud Eisenhower never gave a great deal of thought to her legacy as first lady. Nonetheless, describing herself as a good friend said a great deal about the woman who seemed to be on a first-name basis with the country as "Mamie." She brought a distinctive personality and outlook to the role, and much of her approach was shaped by her experiences as a military wife. Being first lady was a pinnacle of her life, but she was "an army wife" at heart. Twelve years after leaving the White House, she told an interviewer that she and Ike lived their lives grounded in the service. Other first ladies were the wives of generals who ascended to the presidency, but Mamie Eisenhower was the only general's wife to become first lady in the twentieth century. Her experiences were unique among that small sorority of first ladies whose husbands were military men. Mamie, unlike her predecessors, accompanied her husband from one posting to another and to assignments abroad. If Mamie identified with any group of earlier military wives, it was not with former first ladies but with the women who experienced the military frontier of the nineteenth century. "I am proud to feel that they are part of my heritage," she wrote in her introduction to the 1964 reprinting of Lydia Spencer Lane's nineteenth-century memoir, *I Married a Soldier, or Old Days in the Old Army.* In that account, Mamie saw reflections of her own life. The twentieth-century army that Dwight David Eisenhower served had advanced in weaponry and technology, but in many ways, military life for dependents during the first half of the twentieth century had not changed that much from what it had been in the late 1800s. There were frequent moves from post to post, sometimes long separations, and getting by on army pay.[2]

Also unchanged in the military was the distinct social culture that linked a woman's standing to her husband's rank. Protocol at formal dinners and receptions demanded that husbands and wives be received and/or seated not only according to rank but also by date of commission. Wives were very conscious of who "outranked" them in the pecking order. Military wives spoke of "our" career, and that was exactly the partnership they meant to convey. In the military subculture, these women felt very much a part of a career that affected the entire family. Husband and wife were partners. Certainly, a man advanced in rank when he proved himself, and eventually those found incompetent or temperamentally unsuited climbed no higher. Women could not guarantee their husbands' success, but army wives, like Mamie, understood that "with *our* career, a wife plays a very big part." A woman could hold her husband back "if she doesn't measure up, or if she's a trouble maker, a gossiper, or if she doesn't know the proper things to do." When an acquaintance received the rank of brigadier general in 1940, Mamie found it hard to believe because the wife was "simply awful." From Mamie's viewpoint, the man had managed to advance despite his wife. Women were supposed to help their husbands along. Mamie believed that everything she did mattered, whether it was helping to establish a hospital, which she did in Panama, or redecorate an officers' club, as she did at Fort Lewis. The wife, and children, reflected on the man. Mamie told a group of editors and writers in 1952: "As a soldier's wife I learned early in life that pride in personal appearance is not a superficial thing. It rates high on every officer's efficiency report—and his family is part of that report." Mamie firmly saw herself as a partner in Ike's career. Many close to the Eisenhowers believed that she was an invaluable ally. Said one of Eisenhower's presidential speechwriters, "Ike would have been *Colonel* Dwight D. Eisenhower, if it weren't for Mamie."[3]

Mamie Geneva Doud was born on November 14, 1896, in Boone, Iowa, to John Sheldon Doud and Elivera Carlson Doud. She was the second of four daughters. Eleanor was the oldest; Ida Mae, nicknamed "Buster," arrived in 1900; and Mabel Frances, "Mike," was born in 1902. Mamie had her own family endearment—"Puddy." The Doud daughters made up what Mamie liked to describe as a "girl family," as opposed to Ike's "boy family" of brothers.[4]

John Sheldon Doud could trace his family history back to the early 1600s, when the first Doud arrived in America from England. Following the Civil War, John Sheldon Doud's father established a successful meatpacking plant in Chicago, and John received a classical education at Northwestern and Chicago Universities—but not before he took off on a number of adventures, including working as a cook on a Mississippi riverboat. Settling into the family business, John went to Boone in 1893 to work in a company connected to the Chicago-based meatpacking plant. In Boone he met and married Elivera Carlson, whose Swedish parents came to the United States in the late 1860s. Elivera's father was a successful Boone businessman who worked his way up from hired hand at a flour mill to owner. The Carlsons maintained strong ties with family back in Sweden (when Mamie was born, her great-grandmother in Sweden was still living). The Carlsons spoke Swedish at home, displayed photographs of the royal family, and were pious Swedish Evangelicals. Elivera, however, had a mischievous, fun-loving personality that battled with piety, a fact that was not lost on her equally fun-loving daughter. As a child Mamie disliked the trips to church with her

Mamie (left) with two of her sisters, Ida Mae "Buster" and Eleanor.
Dwight D. Eisenhower Library

grandparents. She did not understand the sermons in Swedish, and
then there was the rest of Sunday: "We'd come home and all we
could do was sit on the steps and watch people go by. We couldn't
play cards. We couldn't do anything. . . . It was awful."[5]

John Doud and Elivera Carlson married on August 10, 1894. He
was twenty-four; she was sixteen. They lived in Boone, but less than a
year after Mamie was born, the Douds moved to Cedar Rapids, Iowa.
Mamie's memories of Boone were based on her family's frequent

visits to her Carlson grandparents, but the first home she recalled was in Cedar Rapids. In 1905, the family moved again. Elivera experienced what was described as an emotional and physical "decline." What this actually constituted is unclear, but it was serious enough to require a change of scenery. John Doud moved the family to Colorado Springs. He was in his midthirties but already had a fortune and could look after his family while being semiretired. The choice of location was blamed for new problems, however. Oldest daughter Eleanor developed a serious heart ailment that turned her into an invalid and brought an early death, at the age of seventeen, in 1912. In all probability it was during the family's brief residence in Colorado Springs that Mamie also developed a rheumatic heart condition. The Douds relocated. This time they moved to Denver, where their home was near the city's wealthiest district.[6]

The well-to-do Doud household followed the Victorian family model of the day. Male and female roles were divided into separate spheres of responsibilities. The husband was head of the house, financially supported the family, and made the decisions. The wife ran the house, focused on creating an inviting home life, and was chiefly responsible for child rearing. The Doud household adhered to this basic structure, but it was not as staid as generalities applied to a Victorian home suggests. There was no doubt that John Doud was strict, but he could be quite indulgent when it came to his daughters. Elivera cared very much about propriety and appearance, but she had an infectious sense of humor. Both liked to have fun. On Sunday evenings they held open-house buffets for friends. They played poker and entertained guests in a "recreation room" that contained a piano, pool table, and Victrola. Holidays were grandly celebrated, and birthdays were greeted with great ceremony. The birthday girl led the procession of parents and sisters down the staircase while they sang, inexplicably, "Here Comes the Bride." When the group reached the dining room, the honoree was serenaded with "Happy Birthday" and seated, with a bow from father. Mamie continued this family tradition for some time after she married. "Well here I am 34 yrs old," she wrote her parents in 1930. "Of course we marched and I was the 'bride.'" On another birthday, she recorded an addition to the march—son John playing his harmonica.[7]

The Victorian ideal that young women learn to manage a home, including the servants, and attain social skills suitable to their station held true for Mamie Doud. She took piano and dance lessons. She learned embroidery and sewing. She was intelligent but never a student who excelled at public school. Good grades and outstanding performance were not stressed by her parents. School attendance was occasionally intermittent. She missed almost an entire year because of rheumatic fever, and there were other periods, sometimes months, when the family was away from Denver. Despite these absences, Mamie graduated from eighth grade and moved on to attend high school. That she did so says less about her academic ambitions and more about the era's modern attitude toward secondary education. High school was a relatively new concept in public education. Mamie's attendance reflected both the popular trend of the times and her own family's interest in whatever was modern. The Douds were attracted to anything that smacked of up-to-date ideas and technology. John Doud was particularly interested in the automobile, owned the first in Colorado Springs, and purchased several over the following years, including a 1914 Rauch and Lang Electric Automobile that Elivera claimed as her own and continued to drive for years.[8]

Mamie once told an interviewer, "Most people are raised to do something. I wasn't." In fact, she was educated to be what her well-to-do parents and society expected, a woman with ladylike accomplishments appropriate to her social position. To complete her education, Mamie spent the winter of 1914–1915 enrolled at Miss Wolcott's, a Denver finishing school that advertised itself as a place "for ladies of refinement." She stayed one year. She was more interested in the social life of parties and being called on by some of Denver's most eligible young men. By all accounts, she loved to dance.[9]

Mamie Doud came of age at a time when the rituals and long-held strictures of Victorian culture were being repudiated by an early twentieth-century movement that encouraged women to seek individual freedom and self-expression. The New Woman/Outdoor Girl embodied this movement. The New Woman claimed the right to make her own choices. She might endorse suffrage, seek a college education or professional career, or decide to marry and not work outside the home. The New Woman staked out the right to decide, rather than let social pressures make that decision for her. The independence of the

New Woman was a good fit for Mamie. Although she was hardly a feminist in the way the term was used at the time to suggest a strident suffrage supporter, her personality, and its stubborn streak, naturally sought personal expression. One might add that her younger sister Mike was even more an example of the New Woman. Her nephew John S. D. Eisenhower called her "a true product of the flapper age." She had "an impish sense of humor and a certain abandon" and, despite what others thought or expected, "went her merry way."[10]

A companion to the New Woman was the Outdoor Girl, who refused to stay cloistered at home. She took part in sports, hiked, wore trousers while "roughing it," and explored the world the way a man would. No one would ever claim that Mamie was an Outdoor Girl. She disliked physical exertion, although the Douds and their friends went on camping trips and made excursions into the mountains, where they hiked and fished. After Mamie and Ike met, they spent many days horseback riding and continued to share this interest after they were married. Mamie also took up golf, however briefly, wanting to share her husband's interests and his company. Of one outing she wrote, "Played golf yesterday and was rotten as usual but had a good time," and of a day spent fishing, she proudly wrote her parents, "first fish I ever caught in my life." Generally, however, Mamie did not have the temperament or interests that would make her an Outdoor Girl.[11]

The societal changes introduced by the New Woman/Outdoor Girl benefited Mamie in allowing her more freedom to do things that a respectable young woman would not have done a generation earlier, such as go out unchaperoned or make decisions without seeking parental consent, but she was also very much a product of her social station. After leaving Miss Wolcott's, Mamie did the expected. She made her debut into society. It was the 1915–1916 social season in San Antonio, Texas, where the Douds had wintered since 1910. The Douds had made many friends during their sojourns to Texas, and the wife of Judge Robert P. Ingrum was instrumental in planning Mamie's bow into society. And, it was with the Ingrum family that Mamie first met Dwight D. Eisenhower, a young lieutenant stationed at Fort Sam Houston.[12]

One Sunday afternoon in October 1915, the Doud and Ingrum families visited Judge Ingrum's sister-in-law at Fort Sam Houston.

While they were sitting on the barrack's front porch visiting, two young officers, Leonard T. "Gee" Gerow and Wade H. "Ham" Haislip, joined them. Upon seeing Dwight Eisenhower across the street, they told Mamie that he was "the woman-hater of the post." They called Ike over to be introduced. He complied but was in a hurry to begin his duties as officer of the day. Nevertheless, he noticed Mamie. In his memoirs, Eisenhower later wrote: "The one who attracted my eye instantly was a vivacious and attractive girl, smaller than average, saucy in look about her face and in her whole attitude. If she had been intrigued by my reputation as a woman-hater, I was intrigued by her appearance." She had "clear blue eyes that were full of impertinence." Her "saucy" look and attitude suggested gaiety and playfulness. As Ike noted, Mamie was "smaller than average." Standing just three inches over five feet, she had a small build. In fact, at the age of forty-four she became concerned that her weight of 117 pounds and her twenty-six-inch waist were sure signs of "middle-age spread."[13]

Ike was intrigued with Miss Doud, and Mamie would later say that he was "the handsomest man" she had ever seen. He was far different from the beaus she knew in San Antonio or Denver. When Ike said that he had to make his rounds on the post, Mamie offered to walk with him. "Eventually I found out," Ike wrote, "that one of the things that she was least fond of—to put it mildly—was walking." The young lieutenant began calling on Mamie. When she was off with another admirer, Ike visited with her parents. Finally, Mamie's father told her to "stop her flighty nonsense" or the "Army boy" would quit coming around. Mamie listened.[14]

In January 1916, Ike wrote his longtime friend Ruby Norman in Abilene: "The girl I run around with is named Miss Doud, from Denver. Winters here. Pretty nice—but awful strong for society—which often bores me. But we get along well together—and I'm at her house whenever I'm off duty—whether it's morning—noon—night. Her mother and sisters are fine—and we have lots of fun together."[15]

The rituals and social conventions for courtship were in transition. It was perfectly acceptable for couples to go out alone, unchaperoned. Courtship was moving out of the parlor and into the public world of "dating." For their first date, Ike took Mamie to dinner at the St. Anthony Hotel and then to a vaudeville show at the Majestic

Theater. Ike had more time than money for courting. Later outings were usually dinners at inexpensive restaurants where a meal for two cost about one dollar—with tip. Sometimes they went dancing at the St. Anthony or went to a vaudeville show. "As the winter wore on," wrote Ike, "I became more and more enamored of the girl I had met in October." At Christmas, Eisenhower gave Mamie a heart-shaped, monogrammed jewelry box of sterling silver. (Ike paid for it with money won playing poker.) Mamie's parents insisted she return the gift. It was the sort of personal item that young women received when they were engaged, which Mamie was not. She convinced her parents to let her keep it. As for a formal proposal of marriage, Mamie once said, "We took it for granted that we'd marry." On Valentine's Day 1916, Ike gave Mamie a ring. It was customary for West Point graduates to give their fiancées a miniature of their West Point ring. Mamie did not want a miniature, and Ike had a replica made for her, larger than the traditional engagement ring. When Mamie's father returned from a business trip in March, Ike formally asked for his permission to marry Mamie. The Douds approved the match but asked that the couple wait until November, when Mamie would turn twenty. The Douds thought that the courtship and plans to marry were rushed, but Mamie and Ike considered it "in keeping with the changing customs which were common to their generation."[16]

Not long after Ike obtained the Douds' approval, the engagement was almost derailed. Eisenhower learned that his transfer to aviation, applied for months earlier, had been approved. He was interested in learning to fly, and the extra fifty cents per paycheck was an incentive. His future in-laws were not pleased. John Doud threatened to withdraw his permission if Ike was "so irresponsible to want to get into the flying business." Ike did not immediately respond, but he returned to the Doud home a few days later, saying that he had given up the idea of flying. The Douds were relieved. "Mamie had been raising quite a fuss." Mamie intended to have her way. She knew what flying meant to Ike. She also understood that the couple would have to get along on a lieutenant's salary. Mr. Doud made that clear, cautioning Mamie that there would be no financial help from her family, unless it was a dire emergency. "Well, that didn't make any difference to me," she said. "I wanted that man."[17]

Her will was tested once again when she and Ike decided to move up their wedding date because Ike was unsure of where military operations might take him. In Mexico there was a civil war, and when President Woodrow Wilson refused to recognize the Huerta government in favor of Carranza's claim to the presidency, tensions intensified between the United States and Mexico. Regular army troops and the National Guard were mobilized, and along the U.S. border, rebel Pancho Villa raided towns to protest American interference. General John J. Pershing had the job of leading American troops in the Punitive Expedition to stop Villa. In another part of the world, the United States was not yet fighting the war in Europe, but the army was close to putting itself on readiness alert. Eisenhower did not know how the civil war in Mexico or the European conflict would affect him, but with the future unclear, he and Mamie decided to marry as quickly as possible. The Douds were shocked. What would people say about the abrupt change in plans? Mamie stood firm. "Well," she told them, "Ike is on his way and we have only ten days [to get ready]." He had managed to get leave, and that was that.[18]

Plans to marry in a church service were replaced with a wedding at home. Mamie's dress was store-bought, not custom-made. Ike hastily bought the ring that Mamie already had chosen. On July 1, 1916, Dwight Eisenhower and Mamie Doud were married at noon. They honeymooned at a small resort near Denver, returned to Denver to help address wedding announcements, and then took a train to Abilene for Mamie's first introduction to her in-laws.

It is impossible to know what Ike told his bride about his family and home life. "We were a cheerful and vital family," he wrote later in a memoir. He and his brothers adored their mother, Ida, and respected their father, David. Ike's parents met while attending college in Kansas. Their classical educations included the study of Greek and Latin, and their interest in education was passed on to their sons. So too was the belief in a strong work ethic. If the boys wanted a baseball glove or a football, they had to earn the money to pay for it. The Eisenhower family was not poor in the sense that it was hovering on the brink of poverty, but there was an undercurrent of survival. In the class-conscious town of Abilene, the haves and have-nots were separated by who lived north and south of the railroad tracks. The

Mamie Doud Eisenhower's wedding portrait, 1916.
Dwight D. Eisenhower Presidential Library

south-of-the-tracks Eisenhowers were working-class. Their two-story home was well kept, if somewhat cramped for a family with six boys, but it paled by comparison to the large Victorian homes occupied by the town's prosperous families north of the tracks.[19]

Ike and Mamie's first visit to Abilene was brief. The newlyweds arrived at three in the morning; the train for San Antonio left at eleven that same morning. To welcome the couple, Ida prepared a "monumental fried chicken dinner." Mamie got on well with Ike's parents. Ike's two youngest brothers, Earl and Milton, who were still at home, "were excited about meeting my bride," Ike wrote. "They were almost her age. They were friends instantly." In fact, when Mamie first saw Milton, she impulsively kissed him on the cheek and said, "You must be my new brother. I've always wanted to have a brother!" To this family story, retold over the years, Milton would add, "And I've been her willing slave ever since!"[20]

The trip to Abilene opened Mamie's eyes to how differently she and Ike had grown up. Before leaving home for West Point, Ike saw very little of anything but Kansas. Mamie's family was well traveled. John Doud, said Mamie, was an "inveterate traveler." Mamie had been introduced to society and attended finishing school. After she and Ike married, she worked to make whatever home they occupied a reflection of the manners and etiquette inherent to her upbringing. Their military quarters might be substandard in construction, but there were candles on the dinner table and finger bowls. When son John was growing up, he had a finger bowl, just like the grown-ups, and years later in the White House, recalled granddaughter Susan, Mamie taught her grandchildren "to use finger bowls properly by the time we were three years old." This was not the sort of lifestyle found in the Eisenhowers' Abilene household. Especially surprising to Mamie was the lack of servants and cooks. Mamie found it difficult to comprehend that Ida did without domestic help, other than that provided by her sons. Then, there was the Eisenhowers' attitude toward alcohol, cards, and tobacco. They did not approve. On subsequent visits, Mamie hung out an upstairs window while she smoked, so as not to offend David and Ida. The Eisenhowers treated Mamie like a daughter, but the home that newlywed Mamie began to create for Ike bore little resemblance to his childhood environment. Her insistence on observing such social niceties as finger bowls and candles broadened Eisenhower's view of the way other people lived.[21]

After leaving Abilene and returning to Fort Sam Houston, the couple settled into quarters consisting of two rooms. Wedding money from the Douds helped with the purchase of furniture, but what might have passed for a kitchen went largely unused. At first they ate at the officers' mess, but Mamie found the food so unappetizing, she and Ike began to use the "latest electrical appliances" received as wedding gifts. They purchased a small icebox so that she and Ike "could test our own ability to subsist entirely on our own efforts." Mamie's cooking talents were severely limited. Other than fudge, she had mastered only mayonnaise during the few cooking lessons taken after she became engaged. Ike, on the other hand, had learned to cook at home, helping Ida in the kitchen. Slowly the couple expanded their menus to include pot roast, chicken, and steak. The "meals became so presentable," said Ike, that the couple began to invite friends in for dinner. Adding to their home entertainment was a piano rented with some of the wedding money. Mamie began to replicate, however simply, her family's Sunday night tradition of inviting friends in, and this sort of entertaining became a staple in the Eisenhowers' life. Ike was obviously proud of his new wife as they settled into life at the fort. He later wrote: "Mamie, young, full of life, and attractive was the pet of the post, . . . [she was] showered with attention."[22]

Eisenhower did, however, worry about his bride on the nights he was on duty. On the post, there were clashes between regular army and National Guard troops mobilized for the Punitive Expedition, as well as a number of break-ins. Eisenhower gave Mamie a .45 pistol and taught her to use it. She took the situation seriously, but when Ike decided to test her reaction to someone breaking in, she had to hunt for the pistol. With some amusement, Ike later recalled: "She had the pistol hidden behind the piano, inside a bedding roll, under other possessions, and in general so far buried that she couldn't have gotten it out in a week, much less in a hurry."[23]

Mamie argued with Ike over being left alone. She did not fully understand or realize that Ike steadfastly believed that his duty to the military came first. He was straightforward, and she came to accept his principles, but as a new bride and as the daughter of prosperous parents, she was spoiled enough to expect him to do as she wanted. She had learned at an early age to manipulate her parents, especially her father. If she made a fuss, she usually got her way. She had a temper and sometimes, without thinking, said hurtful things. "Be awfully careful of saying things that offend or hurt," her father once cautioned. "I know that you do not mean any harm but you should watch your little 'clapper.'" Mamie's outbursts did not have the desired effect on Eisenhower. Over time, she learned self-control, but she never gave up expressing herself. She could hold her own with Ike, and did so in private. There were disagreements, but son John had "no memories of the two of them arguing between themselves," other than an occasional complaint from Mamie that Ike brought work home from the office. Things did not always go smoothly between them, but at the core, they had a "loving relationship."[24]

It was during one of Eisenhower's absences—this time sent temporarily to Fort Oglethorpe, Georgia—that Mamie gave birth to their first child. Her mother had come to Fort Sam Houston to help when the baby arrived. When Mamie went into labor, she and Elivera got a ride on the mule-drawn wagon to the post infirmary, which Mamie described as "no place for a mother or babies." Doud Dwight Eisenhower was born September 24, 1917; nicknamed Little Ike, he was soon being called Icky or Ikky (spellings varied). Eisenhower was overjoyed with the news of his son: "Why you sweet little old girl. . . . How I wish I could come and see you and see 'IT.' I'll love the name and Him (no matter what you call him) but most of all, I'll love *YOU.*" The letters that followed were just as ardent: "I love you— love you love you, awful much." Eisenhower did not see Mamie or his new son for almost four months, and then he was granted leave only because Mamie developed a serious case of pneumonia.[25]

The Eisenhowers remained separated until April 1918, when Mamie and Ikky joined Ike at Camp Colt in Gettysburg, Pennsylvania. Housing was difficult to find, and the Eisenhowers packed and moved three times in less than a year. When the armistice ended the war in Europe in November 1918, Ike was reassigned. Soon after, the Eisenhowers received the terrible news that Mamie's sister Ida Mae "Buster" was dead from complications associated with a kidney infection. Ike could not get leave to accompany Mamie to Denver, and their parting, he wrote, was "the most trying we had encountered in our less than three years of married life."[26]

Ike and Mamie were not reunited for any length of time until early in 1920, when Eisenhower was assigned to Fort Meade, Maryland. During the interim, Mamie stayed with the Douds while Eisenhower was posted at Fort Dix and Fort Benning and when he accompanied the 1919 Transcontinental Convoy. When Mamie arrived

Mamie, Ike, and son Doud Dwight "Ikky," 1918; the child died of scarlet fever in
January 1921. Dwight D. Eisenhower Library

at Fort Meade in 1920, she set out to "transform an ancient set of
barracks into a home." The barracks were converted into housing for
officers and their families after troops were demobilized following
World War I. The housing came as it was. Officers had to pay for any
remodeling, and it went without saying that they paid for their own
furnishings. The officers, including the Eisenhowers and their
neighbor George Patton, hired soldiers to tear out walls, install
plumbing, and generally serve as handymen.[27]

The Eisenhowers needed furniture, leaving Mamie to improvise. A dressing table was made out of orange crates. From a "dump pile" left from unused items donated to the Red Cross during the war, Mamie scrounged and came home with a rattan chaise and a table (which she still had when the Eisenhowers moved to the Gettysburg farm in the 1950s). She made drapes from fabric that was really intended for making towels, and she sewed head and foot covers for the army cots they slept on. "That's the nice thing about the service," she once said. "You're not trying to keep up with the Jones' or someone else." Even the Pattons, who were wealthy and could afford the best, were living in the same sort of "old broken-down quarters."[28]

The Eisenhowers saw quite a bit of the Pattons. George Patton and Ike spent many evenings talking tanks, and while Mamie and Bea (Beatrice) Patton never became intimate friends, they were congenial. Some ten years after being neighbors at Fort Meade—and after a number of other postings—Mamie and Bea met for lunch while both were in the Washington area. "We had a good visit," Mamie told her parents. "We don't see them [Pattons] very often— sure like them tho." It was the way of things in the military. You might not see acquaintances or friends for extended periods of time, but the wives formed a network that offered companionship and help when needed. "Oh, but that was the army way," Mamie explained. "You moved in and if it was a hot day, someone brought you over some lemonade, or sheets if your stuff had not arrived, or cooking pans. We all did it."[29]

At Meade, the Eisenhowers suffered what Ike described as "the greatest disappointment and disaster in my life." Three-year-old Doud Dwight became ill with scarlet fever just before Christmas and died on January 2, 1921. The post doctor brought in a specialist from Johns Hopkins, but there was little the doctors could do. "We were completely crushed," said Eisenhower. "For Mamie, the loss was heartbreaking, and her grief in turn would have broken the hardest heart." News of the child's death affected the whole camp. The men of the Tank Corps had adopted the child as a mascot, and many on the post doted on him. The Eisenhowers escorted the small casket back to Denver, where Ikky was buried next to Mamie's sisters Eleanor and Buster. The death of a child can irreparably damage a marriage. The bond between Ike and Mamie held, however, and the grief became part of who they were as a couple. Doud Dwight "Ikky" became an absent presence. "Ike and I spoke of Icky several times on the 24th [his birthday]," Mamie wrote her parents in 1940; on another birth date, she wrote, "To-day is Iky's 26th birthday—hardly seems possible."[30]

Ike and Mamie settled back into life on the post, remaining at Meade until Eisenhower was assigned to Camp Gaillard in the Panama Canal Zone. In 1903 the United States obtained a lease on the Canal Zone. After the canal was completed by the U.S. Army Corps of Engineers in 1914, the United States held a strategic position manned by its troops. Mamie was not happy with the posting. She was already familiar with Panama, thanks to one of her father's lengthy family trips. She felt that she "knew everything about it," and what she knew was not inviting. Ike agreed that it was not the "best introduction to life beyond our borders." The houses were holdovers from the days of canal construction. Mud slides were so common that they were considered more of an inconvenience than a danger, and frequent rains soaked through roofs, walls, and windows. Perhaps the worst part of this tropical life was the infestation of bugs of every sort, as well as lizards, rats, and bats that found their way into homes. In retrospect, Mamie made light comedy out of telling how Ike went after an intruding bat with his sword: "Ike was so grim and earnest, I didn't dare laugh. . . . I kept thinking of Douglas Fairbanks, the great leaper and jumper and swordsman of the movies." The reality, however, was anything but humorous. "Mrs. Conner [wife of the camp's commander General Fox Conner] thought I was a namby-pamby . . . but to have bats crawl in under the door at night and fly around was not my idea of a good time," Mamie later said.[31]

When the Eisenhowers arrived in Panama, Mamie made no secret of her dislike for the place. The living conditions were less than ideal, and she was often unwell, expecting a second child. Virginia Conner took Mamie under her wing. It was part of the army way, but Mrs. Conner also saw how well Ike and General Conner got along, spending hours discussing war, strategy, and the military in general. "I never saw two men more congenial," she said. Virginia wanted to do whatever she could to make Mamie more comfortable and raise her spirits. That particular goal was helped along when Mr. and Mrs. Doud, along with Mamie's sister Mike, came for a visit.[32]

As they prepared to return to the States, it was decided that Mamie would go with them and have the baby in Denver. Mamie needed little urging. The nearest hospital to Camp Gaillard was several miles away, and the only access road crossed one of the canal locks. In an emergency, the hospital might not be reachable for an hour or more. Mamie felt that she had been extremely lucky when Ikky was delivered without complications at the Fort Sam Houston infirmary. She did not want to take the chance in Panama. Ike followed later and was in time for the birth of John Sheldon Doud Eisenhower on August 3, 1922. The Eisenhowers did not consider the boy a replacement for the one they lost, but he "did much to fill the gap that we felt so poignantly." The couple became absorbed with the baby's development into a "walking, talking, running-the-whole household young fellow." Eisenhower went back to Panama three weeks after the birth. Mamie and John followed two months later, with a baby nurse hired by the Douds.[33]

The return brought a difficult episode in Mamie's life. She came to resent the time Ike spent in deep conversations with General Conner, and she worried constantly that the tropical climate would bring some terrible illness to baby John. Mamie's own health suffered, and she began to have digestive problems. Sometime in 1923 she went back to Denver, taking John and the baby nurse. Ike begged her not to go, but she later explained her actions by saying, "I don't know what it was, but there was something about the tropics that got to me. . . . My health and vitality seemed to ebb away." In Denver her health returned, and during the time there, Mamie reflected on herself and her marriage. She saw old friends who had married and were leading the sort of lives that Mamie would have had if she had married a businessman, a lawyer, or doctor. In what can only be described as a defining moment, she realized that she wanted Ike, and that to stay married she would have to adjust to what the military demanded of both of them.[34]

It was a more mature Mamie who returned to Panama. She wrote her parents that she was content and happy. "In fact everything is rosey." John was a delight, the Eisenhowers had a social life of dinners with friends and bridge clubs, and while Ike readied his horse for a big show, he and Mamie rode every morning. Mamie also took on a project that would benefit the camp. It was a "crying shame," she complained to Virginia Conner, that there was no post hospital for child care or maternity patients. The lack especially affected the enlisted men's families, the majority of whom were Puerto Rican. Since the army would not spend the money for a facility, Mrs. Conner got permission to convert a run-down building near the post. Mamie spearheaded the fund-raising. It was not easy. Most everyone barely got by on their pay and could ill afford donating money to the project. Mamie, however, organized bridge tournaments, parties, and dinner dances that raised the $1,000 needed to furnish and remodel the building. Virginia Conner watched Mamie "turn into the person to whom everyone turned. She developed a sure and steady hand."[35]

When the Eisenhowers left Panama in September 1924, Ike went back to Fort Meade. In the next three years, he was posted to Fort Logan, attended the Command and General Staff School at Fort Leavenworth (where he finished first in his class), went to Fort Benning, and then to the American Battle Monuments Commission in Washington, D.C. The commission was mandated by Congress to erect monuments and to establish and maintain cemeteries in Europe for the 120,000 Americans who died there during World War I. The job of creating a guidebook on the European cemeteries and battle sites fell largely to Eisenhower. After completing the guide, within the six months allotted him, Ike attended the Army War College at Fort McNair outside Washington, D.C. After graduation in 1928, he was given the choice of joining the Army General Staff in Washington or going to the Paris headquarters of the American Battle Monuments Commission to work under General Pershing. The commission was collecting additional material for a revised monuments guide. Although Mamie would say many times, in one way or another, that she was "old-fashioned enough" to believe that the man was head of the household and made the decisions, she offered her own opinions on what Ike should do. When it came to staying in Washington or going to Paris, she said, "Honey, let's go to Europe. Let's take this assignment. This gives us an opportunity to see the Old World and travel and everything."[36]

Ike, Mamie, and six-year-old John sailed for France in July 1928. The family took an apartment located on the right bank of the

Seine, about a mile from the Eiffel Tower. The apartment became an informal gathering place for army friends and young officers in Paris. "We have a good poker and heart crowd now," Mamie wrote about the gatherings at what came to be known as "Club Eisenhower." On Christmas 1928, Mamie wrote her parents that "all the gang are coming in this afternoon. . . . I'm glad everyone likes to come here and they all say it is so homey and bright." Just as at their earlier postings, Mamie created an inviting environment that attracted people to her and Ike. Meanwhile, John attended the McJanet School for American Children, and Mamie studied French with a tutor, but she never advanced much beyond the smattering of schoolgirl French she brought to the country. The Eisenhowers seldom sampled Paris nightlife, although on a few occasions they had dinner out or attended the theater. In one instance, Ike wrote the Douds that he and Mamie planned to see "the show that has 'Old Man River' in it—whatever that is."[37]

Ike had heard of the song but was rather vague on the Broadway version of *Show Boat*. His time was taken up with revising the monuments guide and traveling to sites that were to be included. Sometimes Mamie and John went along. After one trip, Eisenhower wrote the Douds that since their trip through France and Belgium, Mamie looked forward to others. Mamie thought the cathedral at Amiens, "the loveliest I've seen." Others scenes were more disturbing. Traveling along what had been the Canadian front lines during World War I, they saw barbed wire, helmets, and trenches still cluttering the fields. It hardly seemed possible after ten years, and Mamie wondered how much more time would pass before the land was reclaimed for farms and villages.[38]

Before returning to the United States, the Eisenhowers decided to see a little more of Europe with their friends Major William Gruber and his wife, Helen. The couples first met while Ike was at Command and General Staff School at Fort Leavenworth. Their driving trip of seventeen days took them through France, Belgium, Germany, and Switzerland. (John was at summer school.) The two couples were good traveling companions and found much to enjoy in the scenery and places they stopped. In the Alps, the women were more terrified than thrilled with the views, however. Both Helen and Mamie hated heights. "After gazing into one of these chasms," Ike wrote in his trip diary, "Mamie suddenly announced that in case she fainted she would like us to know there were smelling salts in her bag! So far we haven't had to use them." Near the end of the trip, Eisenhower wrote that after descending through the Alps, Mamie suffered the "customary" result—a reaction to changes in altitude and an attack of indigestion. Although many people react negatively to mountain altitudes, Ike's notation suggests physical problems of dizziness and stomach upsets that became recurring problems, no matter the location.[39]

The Eisenhowers saw some of the Old World, and Ike completed his assignment with the commission in Europe. When they returned to the United States in 1929, Ike was stationed in Washington at the headquarters of the American Battle Monuments Commission. Then, in late 1929, Eisenhower moved to the office of the assistant secretary of war. In February 1933 he was formally named special assistant to Chief of Staff Douglas MacArthur, although he was already carrying out assignments under MacArthur's direction. In a 1932 letter, Mamie informed the Douds that MacArthur told Ike that he wanted him on his staff. "Surely it was a marvelous compliment to Ike." Eisenhower said much the same thing to his in-laws: "Of course we were flattered that he liked my work well enough to want to keep us." Although Mamie and her family hoped that Ike's next posting would be Fort Sam Houston near San Antonio, MacArthur's offer was too important to refuse. Mamie explained to her parents that to Ike's way of thinking "if any thing should pop in China [where Ike's friend Gee Gerow was assigned] he is on [the] ground floor to hop right off. I think it would kill him if another war broke & he didn't get in it—surely in this man's army we can never tell or make plans."[40]

As a member of MacArthur's staff, Eisenhower was called on to join MacArthur when the general decided to personally oversee federal troops sent to quell the violence that erupted after the Bonus Army, about 15,000 World War I veterans, converged on Washington, D.C. They were demanding payment of promised service bonuses. During the summer of 1932, the veterans, many accompanied by their families, camped out in abandoned buildings and built tent cities. Tensions erupted into rioting. On the day that federal troops moved in, Mamie was occupied with grocery shopping. She had no idea that anything out of the ordinary had occurred until she returned home in the late afternoon and found clothes "from front door back." Ike had hurriedly come home to change into uniform. Military officers in Washington usually went to work dressed in tie and jacket, but the Bonus Army action demanded the uniform. It took more than an hour for Mamie to learn that "Ike had gone as Gen McArthur's [*sic*] aide to quell the riot." After being told that there was no way of knowing when Major Eisenhower would be home, Mamie wrote her parents, "Then, I did get excited." When Ike finally returned and Mamie learned more about the events, she added in her commentary, "Was such a terrific day for heat. When he came in he didn't have a dry rag on & his good uniform soaked. Washington Police could do nothing with the riot altho they (Bonus) were unarmed but what they did with Stones & Bricks was some thing."[41]

The Bonus Army was just one example of the desperation millions of Americans felt during the Great Depression. Mamie was simply grateful that Ike had a job. During the 1920s, especially after Eisenhower became acquainted with a number of prominent businessmen during the 1919 Transcontinental Convoy, he was offered lucrative jobs in the private sector. Committed to the service, he turned them down. The money would have meant living the sort of lifestyle to which Mamie had been accustomed, but she agreed with his decision to stay in the army. She believed that he would be unhappy doing anything else. Some officers did leave, however, and a few tried to persuade Ike to join them "with this firm and that." After many of those former officers lost their jobs during the Depression, Mamie breathed a sigh of relief, thinking what would have happened if Ike had been among them.[42]

Steady employment did not necessarily translate into a good paycheck. As a savings measure, Congress cut military appropriations, which, in turn, meant that the army reduced pay. Ike lost about $50 out of "an already insufficient pay check." Mamie watched the family budget and some forty years later could still recall the amounts spent out of Ike's $391 monthly salary—$154 for rent, $10 for telephone, $5 for an icebox, and $5 a week for Ike's lunches and car fare. There were also the utilities and the expenses of entertaining. Washington protocol demanded perfunctory social calls, and with Ike's position came the expectation that he and Mamie would make the social rounds, as well as entertain fellow officers and superiors. There were dinner parties at home, and occasionally the Eisenhowers hosted dinners at Washington's well-known Willard Hotel. Sometimes the flowers for table decorations cost as much as the food, but Mamie considered flowers integral to a gracious meal, not an extravagance.[43]

Washington, D.C., was the nation's capital, but it was also a small town. In his work, Eisenhower came in contact with other officers, congressmen, and cabinet members. He was not intimidated by the important individuals with whom he associated. Neither was Mamie. Although the Eisenhowers were lower on the social ladder than a cabinet member, Mamie decided that since Secretary of War Patrick J. Hurley and his wife had been kind to them, there was no reason not to return their hospitality by hosting a dinner at the Willard. The Eisenhowers also were invited to the White House, but an invitation to a White House reception "would not have caused excitement around the house," noted son John. The Eisenhowers took it as a matter of course, since one element of the formal social season included receptions for branches of the military and members of the General Staff. Possibly the first such invitation received by the Eisenhowers, since it is the only one saved in Mamie's personal papers, was for a 1932 reception hosted by the Hoover White House. By the time Mamie Eisenhower became first lady, she had been an invited guest in the White House on several occasions.[44]

Mamie was content to stay in Washington, knowing from past experience that the family "could be loads worse off." The Eisenhowers lived at the Wyoming Apartments, where John Eisenhower described them as living comfortably "but far from lavishly." Still, there was a maid; her salary was paid out of $50 a month sent by Mamie's father. Despite his resolution to provide no financial help, other than in an emergency, John Doud routinely did just that. Not long after Ike and Mamie married, Doud bought them a second-hand car. Money sent for Christmas and birthday gifts allowed for the purchase of a few extras, and Doud began a stock portfolio for the Eisenhowers. At least a portion of it survived the stock market crash of 1929, but Mamie was fully aware of how quickly money simply disappeared. Her friend Helen Gruber lost $900 when a Chicago bank failed. The money provided by John Doud for domestic help was greatly appreciated, although Mamie once described that help as "one coming and one going." Living up to Mamie's expectations was not always easy, and Ike seemed resigned to, if not a little bemused by, the turnover. On one occasion he informed Mrs. Doud: "Mamie fired Lulu about four days ago. . . . The same day she picked up another one named Edith." It was a frequent event in the Eisenhower household. "Started a new cook off last Monday," Mamie wrote her parents in October 1930; a month later, it was the same news, "Well, have a new cook to-day." When Mamie was again living at Fort Sam Houston—this time while Ike was on the 1941 Louisiana Maneuvers—she "lost her servants" while trying to entertain and accommodate a number of house guests. Ike shrugged off this latest in domestic news. The two servants, Ike decided, "weren't worth a hoot anyway."[45]

In 1935 the Eisenhowers faced a dramatic change. A year earlier Congress granted commonwealth status to the Philippines, islands acquired by the United States at the end of the Spanish-American War in 1898. The congressional act of 1934 promised that the islands would become an independent nation in 1946. Important to achieving that goal was having an army capable of defending the country. This was critical, particularly in the unstable environment of power shifts in the Far East. By 1934, Japan's ambitions for domination were demonstrated by its invasion of Manchuria and withdrawal (along with Germany) from the League of Nations. To create and train a Filipino army, the United States authorized the U.S. Military Mission to the Philippines. It would operate separately from the U.S. Army and its military bases on the islands. Douglas MacArthur, recently retired as army chief of staff, headed the mission and insisted that Eisenhower, then a colonel, take the position of assistant military adviser.

In late October 1935, Eisenhower arrived in the Philippines, but without his family. Six months earlier, Mamie wrote her parents that "it's just taken for granted that we are to go with the general [MacArthur]." She seemed resigned to leaving the apartment that had been home for seven years, but her reluctance increased as the time for leaving drew closer. Later accounts of this period emphasize that Mamie stayed in Washington so that John could complete eighth grade with friends at a familiar school. Certainly, that was a consideration. So, too, was Mamie's health. A recurring digestive problem was not responding to treatment. There were good reasons not to travel with Ike to the Philippines, but underlying all of them was a depth of fear that simply could not be overcome. Mamie had reconciled herself to Panama, but the prospect of another tropical setting brought out her worst fears. She worried about the climate's effect on her health, and John's, anticipating disaster. "Mamie is so badly frightened (both for Johnnie & herself) at the prospect of going out there [Philippines] that I simply cannot urge her to go," Ike explained to the Douds. He hoped either that she would relent after John finished school in June or that his assignment would be blessedly short. "I can only hope for the best, as the idea of being separated from my family has nothing for me but grief."[46]

Mamie and John traveled to the Philippines in late 1936, almost a year after Ike arrived. John was enrolled at the Bishop Brent School, a boarding school in the mountains at Baguio. At MacArthur's insistence, Ike and Mamie took up residence at the Manila Hotel. The two-room suite was not air-conditioned, and Mamie was fairly miserable in the oppressive heat. "So far the Philippines has not seemed to agree with Mamie," wrote Ike. The physical environment was uncomfortable, and as Susan Eisenhower has noted, the couple's relationship was strained by the months of separation. Much later Ike told a friend, newly assigned to the Philippines, that it was "h___ to be separated so long from families. I was out there a year alone, and I did *not* like it." During the time Mamie remained in Washington, she kept up an active social life, sometimes escorted by male friends. There was never any impropriety, and it never occurred to Mamie that anyone would think so. Possibly she hoped that if she waited long enough, Ike would come home and she would never have to see Manila. Meanwhile, Ike established his own circle of friends with whom he played bridge and golf. A frequent golfing partner was Marian Huff, whose husband was also on MacArthur's staff. Mamie regarded Marian as some sort of rival, which probably explains her interest in taking up golf. Marian, however, was an amiable golfing companion for Ike and nothing more. Eisenhower was quite capable of enjoying the company of the opposite sex without overtones of flirtation or infatuation. He maintained a lifelong friendship, for example, with Abilene school friend Ruby Norman, periodically corresponding with her until her death in 1967.[47]

Mamie felt left out of the social life Ike had built for himself in her absence, and there were disagreements. In a fit of pique, she left Manila to visit John at Baguio. The distance of about 200 miles was actually almost double that, since the drive involved winding mountain roads. By the time Mamie's driver reached Baguio, Mamie was vomiting blood. A stomach vessel had ruptured. At the hospital she fell into a coma, and doctors cautioned Ike, who flew immediately to Baguio, that the situation was life threatening. When the crisis passed, their "disagreements . . . began to disappear." Mamie later confessed to her parents that she "made a terrible mistake in not coming out here with Ike [in 1935]. It's up to me to rectify lots of things." Once again she had to remind herself that life in the military demanded adjustment on her part.[48]

Mamie set about creating the kind of home life they had enjoyed in Washington. Work and home were compartmentalized, and it is difficult to gauge how much Mamie knew about the difficult problems Ike faced. He was often frustrated—and sometimes disgusted—with MacArthur, the work of training and equipping an army from scratch, and finding the money to do the job. Ike did not verbally vent his frustrations at home, however, and John called the years in the Philippines "among the happiest in my life." Mamie and John took advantage of the rare opportunities when they could accompany Ike on inspection tours, and John also traveled alone with Ike. It was the sort of father-son togetherness that Mamie encouraged. She did "everything possible to promote a close relationship between Dad and me," wrote John. As parents, Ike and Mamie were strict, but they were openly proud of their son. Mamie was admittedly overly protective, but John realized that the deaths of Ikky and Mamie's two sisters in a short span of years produced a woman who "tended to be a worrier."[49]

Mamie and Ike took part in the social swirl that was Manila. "[The] social life was terrific," she later said. "You had plenty of that." In just one letter to the Douds, Mamie recounted a luncheon given by army friends, a reception hosted by Philippine vice president Sergio

Ike, Mamie, and son John in the Phillipines, 1937.
Dwight D. Eisenhower Library

Osmeña, and the Eisenhower's own dinner party for ten. "My flow-ers," Mamie wrote, "were 5 huge center pieces of gardenias—They were lovely." The Eisenhowers mixed with the upper echelon of Fili-pino society. They often were invited to dinners, dances, and recep-tions given by Philippine president Quezon, and there were more in-timate get-togethers with army friends. Mamie's closest friends were other military wives. Among them was Jean MacArthur, whose initial arrival and marriage to the general was cause for talk. "We were much surprised over Gen McArthurs [*sic*] marriage," she wrote. "She's a nice person and I think he did right well by himself. We didn't think she'd ever get him tho."[50]

The Eisenhowers briefly returned to the States in 1938. Ike had the difficult job of procuring assistance to arm the Filipino military. For Mamie, the trip meant seeing family but also undergoing surgery for removal of a uterine fibroid. After convalescence in Colorado, she traveled with Ike to Washington in September. Ike had some success in finding aid for the Filipino army, and Mamie was visited daily by numerous friends. It was "fine for her mental attitude," Ike decided.

After the family returned to the Philippines, it was evident that her physical health was much improved, too. For the time spent in the Philippines, most historians, if they notice Mamie at all, have her bedridden and chronically ill. Her letters tell a very different story. Certainly, she was often unwell prior to her surgery in 1938, and the incident at Baguio was a medical emergency. Even during her first two years in the Philippines, however, she was not confined to bed. And after her surgery, her letters reveal an energized, active woman. She was out and about, visiting John, entertaining friends, attending social events, or hosting them.[51]

Upon their return to Manila, the Eisenhowers moved into an air-conditioned apartment in the new wing of the Manila Hotel. Inexplicably, the arrangement angered MacArthur, who had the air-conditioned penthouse. The Eisenhowers' new suite was so extravagant in French decor that Mamie refused to unpack until she was assured that it would cost no more than their earlier accommodations. "You should see the 3 happy Eisenhowers sitting in their Louis Quinze salon. John doing an examination Ike is giving him in Ancient History . . . and me playing solitaire." To her parents, Mamie proclaimed, "I feel very much like Mrs. 'Rich Bitch.'" The words jump from the letter's page. They are so out of character for Mamie. Possibly one of her friends used the term when the Eisenhowers showed off the apartment, or she was just overwhelmed by the "dressy suite." More important than the apartment's elegance, however, was the air-conditioning, which played a very big part in improving Mamie's outlook and general health.[52]

While the Eisenhowers were in the United States during 1938, Ike took the opportunity to contact officers and friends who might help him leave the Philippines. He had extended his time already, allowing President Quezon to persuade him to stay until October 1939. As time went on, Ike became more concerned over his career. He began to discuss the matter with Mamie, and "for practically the only time in my recollection," recalled John, "we held a family council." John believed that his father had made his decision, but talking with his family, listing pros and cons, helped clarify his thoughts. Mamie told Ike that it was his decision to make. She "didn't want any comebacks like the France detail." Although his work with the American Battle Monuments Commission in Europe later served Eisenhower well during World

Mamie pins the Philippine Distinguished Service Cross on Ike during a farewell dinner hosted by Philippine president Manuel Quezon (center).
Dwight D. Eisenhower Library

War II, he generally disliked the duty. Evidently, he more than once blamed Mamie for their decision to go to Paris, and she would not allow that to happen with his decision to go or stay in the Philippines. "I told him," Mamie wrote her parents, "that it has taken me 22 years to find out that the only way I can get along with him is to give him his own way *constantly.*" In truth, Ike did not have to ask if Mamie was willing to go back to the States. There was never a question of that.[53]

In the spring of 1939, Eisenhower received orders to report to Fort Lewis, Washington. The date for return to the United States was set for December 1939. Mamie attended to the packing, telling her parents that it was "a terrible job," since everything they owned had to be inventoried and appraised. At the same time, Ike was in contact with his friend Mark Clark (at that time a lieutenant colonel) at Fort Lewis, asking if someone could measure the windows of their future quarters—Mamie wanted to buy curtain fabric because it was less expensive in Manila than in the States. Clark obliged with the information, adding that their quarters had three bedrooms, two baths, a living room, dining room, maid's room, kitchen, sun room, and sleeping porch. After living in apartments for more than a decade, the Eisenhowers would have a house to call home.[54]

As departure drew near, dozens of farewell parties and dinners toasted the Eisenhowers. President Quezon, who truly hated to see Ike leave, hosted a luncheon to honor the couple and present Ike with the Philippine Distinguished Service Cross. To Mamie's surprise, Quezon gave her the honor of pinning it to Ike's jacket. "You helped him earn it," Quezon told her. On the day of sailing, many friends, both Americans and Filipinos, said good-bye at the ship. "We were made to feel that our going was sincerely regretted in Manila," wrote Ike. Mamie agreed. "We sure went off in a blaze of glory—seemed like all Manila was down to bid us a 'Bon Voyage'—they even had the band down to play us on our way."[55]

The trip home meant stops in Hong Kong, Shanghai, Kobe, Yokohama, and Honolulu. While in Shanghai, Ike noted in his diary: "We are doing some shopping, principally with respect to fur coats, of which Mamie has ordered two. I hope she gets some use out of them." The coats were bargains compared with prices in the States. Later, after arriving in San Francisco, he wrote that Mamie had worn one of her coats "two or three times. . . . I hope that this time her purchases really prove useful; sometimes they're just extra freight." Christmas was spent in Hawaii. Mamie wrote the Douds that "John looked like a million in his new dinner jacket. It would have made your heart swell with pride. . . . Ike and I were overcome." Mamie was in a happy frame of mind, but as the ship carried them to the United States, she wrote that she left behind "some good friends" in the Philippines.[56]

CHAPTER 2

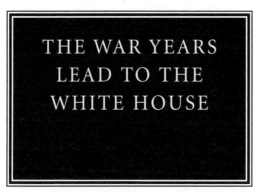

THE WAR YEARS
LEAD TO THE
WHITE HOUSE

On December 7, 1941, Ike worked in the morning, went home, and decided to take an afternoon nap. Mamie woke him with the news of the Japanese attack at Pearl Harbor. The Eisenhowers were now at Fort Sam Houston. Ike's posting of about seventeen months at Fort Lewis, Washington, ended in June 1941, and by July, Ike wrote an old friend that "shipping troubles were a bit worse than usual [many pieces of furniture were damaged], but here we are!" Ike and Mamie celebrated their twenty-fifth wedding anniversary at the post where they began married life.[1]

Ike's return to Texas brought an important event in his career. He participated in the Louisiana Maneuvers, a military exercise designed to evaluate army readiness and officer capability. Eisenhower's planning and organizational skills were well known among his peers. Now they attracted attention from the upper echelon, including Chief of Staff George Marshall. At the conclusion of maneuvers, Eisenhower received his first general's star. Mamie later said that the day "he got his first star was my biggest thrill. . . . The first one is always the biggest one." Ike tried to downplay his own pride by telling a friend that Mamie "has found out that I don't get a red cent with all this new glory—but she has to dole out to tailors some hundred and fifty bucks just to change over uniforms. She's been punch-drunk ever since learning all this."[2]

Five days after Pearl Harbor, Eisenhower was ordered to Washington and the War Department. He was told to get there as soon as possible. Mamie packed his bag, and he was gone. She wrote her parents that they were "lucky" that Ike was in Washington "instead of out in the wilds some place." The couple had no idea what the future held, but in the immediate present, Mamie was determined to go ahead with the plans she and Ike had made to spend Christmas vacation at West Point, where John was a plebe. Mamie spent the holidays with John, "proud as a peacock over my son." Ike's heavy workload kept him in Washington, where his first responsibilities at the War Department involved operations in the Philippines. The Japanese began making small landings on December 10, 1941. On December 22 a force of 43,000 landed. Within ten days, Manila was in Japanese hands. By the end of December, American forces had fallen back to the Bataan Peninsula. Mamie, who joined Ike in Washington, was caught up in the wrenching drama of friends and acquaintances trying to learn what had become of their loved ones. Among them was one of Mamie's friends from their Philippine days. "Poor Kitty Smith," wrote Mamie, "arrived in Washington . . . to see if she could get any word of Howard—apparently no one can get any news of Manila or casualty lists—We should feel mighty lucky that we are all in this country—Poor things who have sons & husbands in the P.I."[3]

During the brief time spent together over the holidays, the Eisenhowers decided that Mamie would move to Washington. She returned to Fort Sam Houston and began packing the family's possessions, accumulated during twenty-five years of marriage. Furniture (including a Chinese folding screen, a china closet, and at least fifteen tables of various sorts), rugs (which had to be mothproofed), china, silver, crystal, and everyday household goods had to be itemized, packed, and crated. Most of the possessions went into storage and were not seen again until the 1950s, when the Eisenhowers completed their house at Gettysburg.[4]

Upon her return to Washington, Mamie wrote her parents, "The city is a mad house." People were coming into Washington at such a pace that housing was at a premium. The Eisenhowers were welcome to stay with Ike's brother Milton and his wife, Helen, but that was a short-term solution. Mamie had to find an apartment. "I feel like a football—kicked from place to place," she told the Douds. Harry Butcher, a vice president of CBS in Washington and later on Ike's staff in Europe, located an apartment at the Wardman Park Hotel. Compared with the generous quarters Mamie had just vacated at Fort Sam Houston, the apartment was small—one bedroom, living room, bath, and kitchenette. Still, she was glad to be with Ike, and "Poor Ike seems so pleased to have me [here]." He was working "terrible" hours, and Mamie set about creating for Ike "his own home" where he could relax and get away from the pressures of his job. She saw this as a primary responsibility of a homemaker and took the word in its truest sense, making a home, not simply keeping one.[5]

Making a home meant creating an atmosphere that made the home a refuge where her husband could escape the huge demands that he faced in the outside world. "No matter how humble your house," she once wrote a woman who asked for advice, "you can give it a peacefulness and cleanliness making it a haven for your husband at the end of a long day's work." The home-as-refuge was a model of family life that Mamie strongly maintained. When Ike came home, she did not meet him at the door ready to tell him whatever daily problems she encountered in running the household. Conversely, "when he came home, he was home and we didn't discuss what his big problems were." She later told an interviewer, "That was the way we managed our lives."[6]

While Ike put in long hours at the War Department, Mamie quickly became involved in war work. "I am chairman of my group at Soldiers, Sailors & Marine Club canteen," she told her parents in April 1942. She volunteered with the Army Relief Society, American Women's Volunteer Service, and the United Service Organization (USO). She had worked for the American Red Cross at Fort Lewis and Fort Sam Houston and continued to do so in Washington. While visiting friends in New York in the early fall of 1942, she was invited to be a hostess at the Stage Door Canteen. Mamie enthusiastically agreed, writing her parents, "[I] think it will be fun."[7]

Whether pouring coffee during her shifts at the canteen in Washington or doing other volunteer work, Mamie did not draw attention to herself. This was not the case for other military wives, notably Bea Patton and Maurine Clark. Mamie had known Bea since the Pattons were their neighbors at Camp Meade. She became well

Mamie in the uniform of the American Women's Volunteer Service;
behind her is a photo of Ike. Dwight D. Eisenhower Library

acquainted with Maurine, wife of Mark Clark, while the Eisenhowers were at Fort Lewis, and both Eisenhowers were touched by how
thoughtful and helpful the Clarks had been to them and John during that time. Bea Patton and the outgoing and attractive Maurine
Clark became public figures when they joined a bond-selling show
that traveled the country. Maurine Clark was especially active. Several months during each year of the war, she made speeches at rallies
and shows that included such entertainers as Glenn Miller. Mamie

avoided this sort of limelight. When she volunteered, she tried to keep her identity concealed. Only her closest friends knew the extent of her volunteer work, and only her family knew that she used her own savings and money sent from her father to buy bonds. By late fall 1943, she informed the Douds: "Now I have over $10,000 in bonds." When a longtime friend from San Antonio asked permission to auction off one of Ike's old raincoats for a war loan drive, she agreed with some amusement. To the outside observer, however, Mamie seemed aloof from the volunteer work other military wives were doing, and she was criticized for her lack of participation.[8]

Time spent at the Wardman was short. General Marshall wanted his staff headquartered at Fort Myer. By April 1942, the Eisenhowers moved to Myer, but the couple was barely settled when Ike was named commanding general of U.S. Army forces in Europe. John Eisenhower later said that he was "mildly startled" when he heard the news. He was well aware that his father was respected for his organizational and planning skills, but "the command of a theater of war—potentially the major theater—was almost too much to comprehend." On June 21, 1942, Eisenhower and Mark Clark saw Roosevelt and Winston Churchill at the White House. Afterward, Ike returned to the quarters at Fort Myer. John had been allowed a few hours away from West Point to be with his father before he left for Europe. "The atmosphere among the three of us was sober but hardly sad," John recalled. Mamie stepped back, allowing father and son time together. Two days later, Eisenhower was on his way. He asked Mamie not to come to the airfield to see him off, but to stand by the flagpole at Fort Myer so that he could see her as the plane flew over. He kissed her on the head and said, "Goodbye, Honey." There was no way to foresee how long Ike would be gone. Perhaps the only thing Mamie knew with certainty was that she had seven days to move. Years later, she told an interviewer, "They ordered Ike away and I was ordered off the post." Military dependents were not allowed to remain in post quarters when their husbands were assigned elsewhere. She had to find another place to live. Although she was tempted to do as her parents wanted and come to Denver, she decided to stay in Washington. She wanted to be close if Ike made any trips back to the States. There were also the many friends she had in the city, and she would be able to go to West Point and visit John.[9]

Not long after Ike arrived in England, Everett Hughes, a longtime Eisenhower friend and deputy chief of staff at Ike's headquarters, returned briefly to the States. He passed on the latest news to Mamie. Ike was apparently "taking London by storm." Closer to home, her husband was being celebrated in his home state. Mamie wrote her parents, "Last Friday was 'Hero's Day' in Kansas so Abilene had 'Gen. Eisenhower Day.' Wasn't that cute?" Letters began to arrive from well-wishers, as well as occasional requests that Mamie use her influence with Ike for special treatment or consideration. She did not bother him with the favor seekers, but throughout the war years, she acknowledged every letter received. Sometimes it seemed an impossible task. She told her parents, "I write & write and still the old stack of letters seems to stay the same."[10]

Eisenhower was becoming a household name, but his name recognition was of little help as Mamie searched for a place to live. Washington and its environs saw a population jump of at least 70,000 during the first year of the war. Government employment more than doubled, and an estimated 5,000 new federal workers arrived every month during the first months of the war. Apartment buildings, boardinghouses, and hotels were jammed. Once again, Harry Butcher came to Mamie's rescue. She could share an apartment at the Wardman with Harry's wife, Ruth, and their school-age daughter.[11]

Mamie moved back to the Wardman, trying to keep a low profile as the press increasingly sought her out. The wife of the American commander in the European theater of war was news. "Reporters are here every day taking up at least 2 to 3 hours of my time," Mamie wrote her parents, "another due here in few minutes. Milton sees them all too but guess they like to see what type of person I am." Quite aware of the impression she left with reporters, she was gracious but cautious. Ike sympathized, writing his in-laws that Mamie was "paying one of the penalties of having her family name in the newspapers. My mother has had it, as well as my brothers, although, of course none in the same degree that Mamie has it." Anyone who knew Eisenhower became at least minor news. "So many people are riding on Ike's coat tails these days one more or less doesn't matter," Mamie told her parents. When a Chicago newspaper ran a story on an old girlfriend from Ike's West Point days, Mamie was amused to read the woman's account of "what a marvelous beau he made."

With each victory, and then when Eisenhower was named Supreme Allied Commander, the press sought out Mamie. Photographers gathered in the hotel lobby. Reporters waited outside the elevators. Some came to the door or telephoned. When, at the insistence of friends, she went to Florida for her health in 1945, the press met her at the train. "Was I *mad* after all the precautions we took that no one would know where I'd gone—of course the picture was terrible and plastered on front page of Miami papers."[12]

Soon after Eisenhower went to Europe, a *Washington Post* article gave the public one of its first images of Mrs. Eisenhower. The reporter described her as hospitable, witty, and "wrenlike." The reporter's references to the Eisenhowers' reputation for entertaining, including the days when their Paris apartment was "Club Eisenhower," probably came from Ruth Butcher or one of Mamie's other friends. Mamie's focus was on Ike. "Very slowly," the *Post* writer noted, "the visitor begins to realize" that the conversation always turned away from the subject of Mrs. Eisenhower. A picture accompanying the article showed Mamie standing to one side of a framed photograph of her husband; rather than facing straight into the camera, she looked seriously to one side. The reporter understood that Mamie's poise and words were intended to set an example for all those who like her waited at home.[13]

"One realizes that she has a most remarkable self-control," said the *Post*, "for never by word or sign does she indicate that there is any strain for her in the separation. She speaks not of 'me' or 'my home,' but of 'we' and 'our home,' and her whole attitude would give the impression that 'Ike' is just away for a weekend trip, or on a brief maneuver."[14]

Mamie kept her worries and concerns private. As the wife of the American commander, she was thrust into the sort of role Virginia Conner had once played to a young Mamie in Panama. She offered comfort and support to other military wives, and more than one woman would later recall the way Mamie stayed strong, offering a sympathetic ear to their worries. And, when she thought it necessary, she quietly gave advice. In one instance, a distraught woman at one of the ladies' "hen parties" said, "Well, Mamie, you don't have to worry, because your husband is a general." Later, away from the others, Mamie told her that no one was safe in a war. "Never let me hear you complain about anything, because your husband is a professional soldier and we're the ones who have to hold up. We're the ones who can't complain." She said much the same thing to her sister Mike, whose husband was bound overseas. "I could smack Mike for crying," Mamie told her parents. "Poor kid, it is hard, but I've seen so many other gals left behind too."[15]

Conscious of public perceptions, she seldom went out to parties or dinners. Mamie had no intention of giving the impression of being a gadabout, enjoying Washington nightlife when others were making personal sacrifices during the war. Still, the invitations came. Washington had always been a town of socialite hostesses, embassy parties, and any number of receptions and dinners hosted by government and military officials. "Social competition and social climbing," wrote David Brinkley, "were not invented in Washington in WWII, but they did seem to have been raised—or lowered—to the level of trench warfare." For those to whom such things mattered, entertaining became a competitive sport. "For the ambitious hostess," said Brinkley, "no effort . . . was too great . . . to entice celebrities to their tables, seemingly in the belief that the next best thing to being a celebrity was to feed one." Hostesses sought out exiled European royalty who took sanctuary in Washington, Hollywood stars in town for bond drives, and industrial leaders who arrived in the city on business. Whether she liked it or not, Mamie was in her own small way a celebrity, but she refused to be pulled into the city's social life. Responding to an invitation for dinner at the Shoreham, Mamie simply told the hostess not to expect her. The fact that another guest was a high-ranking official from Ireland impressed her not at all. In a letter to her parents, Mamie confessed that she had no interest in going out, unless it was with her "gang" — her close friends—and even those occasions were rare. In 1943, for example, Mamie dined only twice with her friends at the Army Navy Club. "I never went to a night club," she later told an interviewer. "I just didn't think it was right that *I* should go. . . . other people were suffering over there and my husband was head of it."[16]

Mamie and her friends kept each other company, playing cards and mah-jongg. The women pooled their ration cards to make "decent" meals, but even when they shared their red points—used to purchase meat and butter—they had "a heck of a time" making them go very far. When birthdays and anniversaries came along, they were celebrated "just as if the men were home." Outside this group, Mamie also had Helen and Milton Eisenhower close by. Milton held a number of posts, but for most of the war he was an associate director of the Office of War Information. Beyond these friends, Mamie's outside associations usually took the form of invitations that could not be ignored. On one occasion, for example, she accompanied Ilo Wallace, wife of the vice president, to hear Mrs. Chiang Kai-shek speak before the Senate. On another, she accepted an invitation to a tea hosted by a woman whose son was serving under Ike; former first lady Edith Wilson, who Mamie described as "a great friend," was also in attendance. On the other hand, Mamie declined an invitation to lunch with Eleanor Roosevelt. It coincided with the beginning of John's vacation break at West Point, and nothing outweighed Mamie's determination to spend time with her son. Eleanor did not pursue the invitation for another time, and Mamie did not count her among her friends, as she did Edith Wilson. In fact, when Mamie became first lady, the *New York Herald Tribune* broached the idea of Mrs. Eisenhower writing a daily piece, "An Incident a Day in the Life of the First Lady." Mamie declined: "It sounds like a terrible chore and smacks of [Eleanor Roosevelt's] 'My Day' column, of which I have a perfect horror."[17]

In early 1943, Mamie and Ruth Butcher agreed that their living arrangement was due for a change. Ruth and her daughter were inconvenienced by the reporters who hung around the door waiting for Mamie, and Ruth's friends, both male and female, often congregated at the apartment. Mamie did not know Ruth's acquaintances, putting her in the uncomfortable position of being with people she did not wholeheartedly trust. Mamie realized that Ruth's frequent cocktail parties could hurt her image and, by association, Ike's. Milton, protective of both his brother and Mamie, agreed. "I told her to be careful," he later said. "Not about drinking too much—because she didn't—but about drinking in front of those . . . miserable gals." When Ruth moved to a nearby apartment in the Wardman, it was a mutual decision, and the two women remained friends. The new arrangement "will be for the best," Mamie told her parents. Now they would not be "under each others feet."[18]

Although Mamie and Ruth no longer shared an apartment, their friendship and Ruth's reputation for giving cocktail parties fueled rumors that Mamie drank to excess. Women who envied Mamie for her husband's position were only too happy to suggest that Mrs. Eisenhower's infrequent social appearances were not a sign of devotion to her husband and the war effort, but proof of a serious drinking problem. The whispers got back to Mamie, and like most subjects, she discussed it with her parents. Drinking was not her habit, she told them, but alcohol was the habit of Washington's social climate. Mamie was not a teetotaler, but neither was she an alcoholic. Her friends knew that the rumors were false. Most important, Ike knew. She would never have done, by action or word, something that would have compromised their personal relationship or the difficult job that faced her husband.[19]

Health problems added to the whispers. While waiting tables one day at the Soldiers, Sailors and Marines Canteen, she realized that she could not stand. "I was pitching like I used to do in the Philippines." Mamie was suffering from Ménière's disease, although the dizziness and loss of equilibrium would not be diagnosed for some time. The inner-ear disorder produces episodes of dizziness, vertigo, and/or ringing in the ears. There is a sensation of everything moving. With the loss of equilibrium, sufferers might walk into a doorjamb, rather than through the doorway, or find it next to impossible to navigate down a flight of stairs. To the casual observer, someone with Ménière's can appear intoxicated. For Mamie, the attacks became more acute than anything experienced in the Philippines. Sometimes she could not stand or walk. "I crawled on my hands and knees from my bedroom to the kitchen. I didn't dare try to walk—I couldn't walk." Up until the time of these episodes, Mamie had been keeping house by herself, but as the attacks increased in number and intensity, she asked the Reverend Lightfoot Solomon Michaux for help. It is doubtful that Mamie knew Michaux personally, but she certainly knew of him. A well-known radio evangelist, Michaux was an African American leader in the Washington area. Probably better than anyone, he would know where to find domestic help at a time when women were being pulled into industrial and government war work. He sent a woman named Mary Newton, telling her that her contribution to the war effort was to help Mrs. Eisenhower. Later, when Mamie was first lady, one of her many charitable contributions went to Michaux's church; at the same time, and in light of the man's influence in the black community, President Eisenhower (along with Harry Butcher) accepted "honorary deacon" status in the man's church.[20]

The problems with equilibrium curtailed Mamie's volunteer work, leaving her more isolated. Meanwhile, worry and stress, particularly when the war news was bleak, brought on other problems. Chronic stomach problems returned, and she lost weight. She began to suffer severe headaches and insomnia. It was the "quietness" that kept her awake, she said. "I could not stand this absolute loneliness." Ike was away. So was John. Years later she told an interviewer that the only time she got a good night's sleep was when one of her friends stayed the night. Often the friends were Ann Nevins and Louise Caffey, both of whom were army wives and had been Mamie's close friends in the Philippines.[21]

Adding to Mamie's feelings of isolation were stories circulating about Kay Summersby. Washington loves gossip, and the attractive young woman pictured in *Life* magazine, along with seven others on Ike's personal staff, had tongues wagging. Summersby, who volunteered for the British Motor Transport Corps, became one of Ike's drivers. Commissioned ex officio into the Women's Army Corps (WAC) contingent at headquarters, she also acted as his appointments secretary, deftly handling the military and political egos that demanded time with General Eisenhower. When the command went to North Africa, *Life*'s "pretty Irish girl" was conspicuously visible, driving Ike from one place to another. Roosevelt returned from Algiers convinced that there was a romance. He passed on the delicious morsel of gossip to his daughter Anna, adding that even Franklin Jr., who accompanied his father to Casablanca, "fell" for Summersby before deciding that she was "unstable."[22]

Kay was likable and outgoing, but she was hardly the only uniformed female in North Africa. There was a group of WACs attached to Ike's command post, and if someone wanted a truly newsworthy item, these women fit the bill as the first WACs working in a combat zone. Mamie's letters to Ike are not extant, but his letters suggest that she commented on the *Life* piece. Not only had she seen the story, but photographer Margaret Bourke-White visited Mamie when she returned from North Africa. She wanted Mamie to know that she had seen Ike and that he had been "wonderful to her." From his side of the world, Ike informed Mamie that Kay's fiancé, an American colonel named Richard Arnold, was in North Africa. "I doubt that *Life* wrote that," he said. In another letter he wrote: "I just want to say that you're the greatest gal in the world. I'll never be in love with anyone but you! So please be *sure* of that." And, to the Douds he simply wrote, "God, how I miss Mamie!!"[23]

When Summersby's fiancé was killed in Tunisia, Ike and others at headquarters took it upon themselves to help her through that devastating time in her life. Continuing to do her job seemed to be the answer. Later, in the summer of 1944 when the Allies were advancing into western Europe, Ike arranged for Kay, along with others, to take a brief trip to the States. Mamie invited her to the Wardman, where Summersby met other women whose husbands she knew. They wanted to hear how their husbands were—how they looked, their state of health. "It was a lovely afternoon and I enjoyed it thoroughly," Summersby later wrote. She went sightseeing in Washington, shopped for items that were unavailable in bombed-out London, and contacted Arnold's mother. John Eisenhower, newly graduated from West Point, took her sightseeing in New York. The trip displeased Mamie for the simple reason that she wanted her son to herself before he was assigned overseas. Summersby detailed her trip to the United States in her 1948 book *Eisenhower Was My Boss,* adding that she was shocked when she met other military wives and realized that some of the women "gauged each other purely by rank" and believed that "any uniformed female overseas . . . [was] a camp follower." That characterization applied to Kay, too. "I was even more upset at learning my own reputation was lost. I was a *foreign* woman—and I traveled with the High Brass. Therefore, I was a Bad Woman."[24]

Summersby went back to Ike's headquarters. When he returned to the United States in 1946, she was in Berlin as an aide to General Lucius Clay. Kay then came to the United States and became a U.S. citizen. Arriving in Washington, she hoped to get a job at the Pentagon, but was refused. She tried to reconnect with people she had known in Europe, but they were getting on with their lives in the postwar world. She became engaged and then broke it off. When a friend passed along the news to Ike, he could only conclude that she had never gotten over Arnold. Summersby then decided to write a book.

She was not the only person close to Ike to do so; Harry Butcher's *My Three Years with Eisenhower* and Mickey McKeogh's *Sgt. Mickey and General Ike*, as examples, came out in 1946. To garner interest for her upcoming publication, Summersby wrote an article for *Time* magazine providing a preview of titillating snippets such as a cocktail party with General George Patton, as well as her introduction to the Roosevelt boys—Elliott and Franklin Jr.—at Casablanca. There was relatively little about Ike in the article, but Mamie's response was direct: "She has to write something that will sell."[25]

The selling point of *Eisenhower Was My Boss* was not a romance between Kay and Ike. In fact, that was not mentioned until Summersby's *Past Forgetting*, which was written with a ghostwriter and published shortly after Summersby's death in 1975. Still, some have told the story as substantiated fact, citing as proof Truman's allegation that there was a "lost" letter in which Ike told Marshall he was getting a divorce. Others have used Summersby's book as primary source. Those close to Eisenhower and Summersby flatly stated, however, that there was no affair. Sergeant Mickey McKeogh (who put Ike to bed at night and got him up in the morning) and Captain Sue Sarafian Jehl (Kay's wartime friend and roommate) refuted the claim. So, too, did Sir James Gault, General Mark Clark, and the executor of Summersby's estate, who found nothing in her possessions related to Eisenhower, only the love letters written by long-dead fiancé, Richard Arnold. As for Mamie, she was hurt by the gossip, and she was probably jealous of Summersby, not as a rival for Ike's affections but as someone who filled the role she should have played, taking Ike's mind off work by playing cards or horseback riding. At the end of the day, however, Mamie was absolutely certain that Ike had been faithful to her.[26]

There were times when Mamie felt left out and neglected. There was so much that her husband could not tell her. "Everything I do, or see, or hear, or even think, is secret," Ike wrote. Mickey McKeogh corresponded with Mamie every two weeks or so, telling her how Ike was doing, and there were occasional surprises, such as the letter from her brother-in-law Gordon Moore. He had seen her "boy friend." Ike looked fine, reported Moore, but he was very lonely for Mamie. These sorts of letters and those from Ike were Mamie's lifeline to her husband. Official channels were far less informative.

"The War Department gave me *absolutely* nothing," she later said. The exception was Chief of Staff Marshall, who made a point of telephoning her after his trips overseas. After one such call, Mamie confided to her parents, "The 4th [general's] star should come along in the near future. After Tunisia is taken I think—Gen Marshall called me as soon as he returned." Marshall also kept her updated on Ike's health and anything else that did not conflict with security.[27]

The question remained. When would Mamie see Ike? There were suggestions at one time or another that he would return to Washington for conferences with Roosevelt and/or Marshall, but it was not until early January 1944 that he flew home for a brief time. He and Mamie spent a few days at White Sulphur Springs, West Virginia, for privacy, and with the stealth usually employed in spy novels, they visited John at West Point. Mamie, outwardly a tower of strength, had patiently waited for Ike to come home, but she was unprepared for how quickly their time together ended. "He was called hither and yon and every place," she complained. The last straw may have been Roosevelt's insistence that Ike spend his last night in the United States at the White House. Mamie thought that the time with Ike should have been hers. From her point of view, Roosevelt acted thoughtlessly, since it appeared that not all of the evening's conversation concerned weighty matters of war. Mrs. Roosevelt even popped in to say a few words. Upon his return to Europe, Ike tried to smooth hurt feelings, writing that he was glad that he had come home, "even though things did seem to be a bit upsetting." Ike chalked it up to not being able to get reacquainted before he had to leave again. He and Mamie apologized to each other long-distance. After receiving Mamie's third letter since his return to London, Ike wrote that his trip home had "paid dividends." Her letter was "quite the nicest you've written since I left home in June '42."[28]

When Ike returned to England, Mamie went to San Antonio to stay with her sister. She did not return to Washington until the spring, when John graduated from West Point in June 1944. For some time, there had been speculation surrounding an invasion of Europe. No one knew when it was coming, but there was a sense that it would occur sooner rather than later. On June 5, 1944, Mamie arrived at West Point for John's graduation. The Douds were there, too, along with Ruth Butcher and her daughter. On the morning of June 6,

In the summer of 1944, not long after D-Day, Mamie was photographed at
Camp Lee, Virginia, with friends Marge Clay and Mary Horkan.
Dwight D. Eisenhower Library

Mamie was awakened by a telephone call. A reporter wanted to know her reaction to the Allied invasion of German-occupied France. That was how she learned the news. John was told by a classmate. He and his mother were mobbed by reporters and well-wishers throughout the day. Newly graduated from West Point, John had a three-week leave before reporting for duty. Mamie assumed that John would spend the time with her, but Ike wrote that he had "cooked up" something. He wanted to see his son and received permission from Marshall to bring John over.[29]

When John returned to the States, he prepared for overseas duty. Mamie deeply felt that his impending departure would leave her completely alone. She berated Ike for not using his position to change John's assignment with the U.S. First Army in Europe. Mamie accused her husband of playing "dirty tricks" on her. The self-possessed, in-control image that Mamie presented to the world was crumbling. The strain of being away from Ike for almost three years, the Washington rumor mill, and finally her son's imminent departure tumbled out in a letter. Ike's response was measured but stern. He would not interfere with their son's assignment because John would resent it "for the remainder of his life." As for the "beating" that she was taking at home, she had to remember that he took "a beating every day" and constantly received letters from women "begging me to send their men home or, at least outside the battle zone, to a place of comparative safety." Ike ended the letter by telling Mamie that he loved her and that he knew "when you blow off steam you don't really think of me as such a black hearted creature as your language implies."[30]

V-E Day, Victory in Europe Day, came on May 8, 1945. At the time Mamie was in Florida, hoping that the change in scenery would improve her health. Within hours of the announcement that the war was over in Europe, her hotel was mobbed. The news was wonderful, but Mamie had no illusions that Ike would soon be home. When he was given command of the occupation forces in Germany, Mamie astutely understood the situation. "There really isn't any job in the US for anyone [of] his rank till Marshall leaves as chief of staff which he will not do till V.J. day [Victory over Japan Day]. . . . I'm sure Ike will come home in next few months." He briefly returned to the States in the summer of 1945. Beforehand, he wrote that he assumed "when I get home for a visit I'll have to go through some formalities at various places."[31]

If anything, that was an understatement. There were parades in Washington, New York City, West Point, Kansas City, and Ike's hometown of Abilene. "To thousands of people in the crowd," wrote McKeogh of the New York parade, "this was, like the war had been, something that was happening to everyone and when a lot of those people saw the Boss riding up Broadway . . . it was really their own soldiers they were waving and yelling at." After the parade, McKeogh made his way back to the Eisenhowers' suite at the Waldorf. Mamie was preparing for a luncheon. McKeogh described her as "happy and excited and trying to do a hundred things at once." The reception in Abilene was just as heartfelt. "Everything they did seemed . . . more sincere and down to earth. For one thing the General didn't parade in Abilene. He sat on a stand and the town paraded for him—and cheered and waved when it went by." After the parades and cheers, Ike and Mamie had a private week together at White Sulphur Springs. Then he was gone. Waiting for him to be recalled from Germany was a trial. "Still no news of when Ike will be home," Mamie wrote her parents in October 1945. "I'm getting jittery waiting." To keep occupied she spent a great deal of time answering letters, and she read the galley sheets for the Kenneth Davis biography of Eisenhower published in late 1945. Ike finally came home in November. Soon after, Marshall retired, and General Eisenhower became the new army chief of staff.[32]

Eisenhower's position was the ultimate conclusion of any military career, but he had "no personal enthusiasm" for what the job entailed, chiefly demobilization of a wartime army spread around the world. Nevertheless, it was a position that neither he nor Mamie could have imagined in 1916 when they began "their" career at Fort Sam Houston. When Ike became chief of staff, the couple moved into Quarters # 1 at Fort Myer, but over the course of the next two years there was extensive travel. Mamie joined her husband for some of these trips, agreeing to do something that she hated—go by airplane. In Brazil they were decorated by the government. In Scotland, the Scottish Trust gave Ike lifetime use of Culzean Castle's top floor, and the Eisenhowers were guests of the royal family at Balmoral Castle. In London, Queen Mary, the queen mother, received them for tea.[33]

Not long after V-E Day, Mamie wrote her parents: "Well now that things are over in Europe our popularity will dwindle." It was a wishful hope that when Ike came home they could return to quiet anonymity. The reality was very different. Wherever Ike went, people wanted to shake his hand or speak to him. Even a glimpse was enough. At the Broadway opening of *South Pacific,* the Eisenhowers were mobbed inside the theater and as they tried to leave by the back door after the performance. When Virginia Conner invited the couple out for dinner, Mamie suggested that they arrange for a private get-together "because the public won't let Ike eat." They had been to the Shoreham, and so many people crowded around the table that the manager had to use the microphone on the bandstand to ask people to kindly disperse. After that episode, the Eisenhowers decided that there would be no more public meals.[34]

*Ike and Mamie at her fifty-first birthday party in 1947; the fur coat was a gift
from Ike who, at the time, was army chief of staff.*
Dwight D. Eisenhower Library

As retirement from the military loomed, Eisenhower considered his
choices. There was talk of a run for political office. When he was
approached on the subject, he said that he was not interested. He
was offered jobs in the corporate world as a company president or
chairman of the board, but he refused. His idea of retirement, and
one that he discussed with Mamie, was to go to a "little college
town." He was thinking along the lines of being president of a small
college. When he was approached by the trustees of Columbia
University, his first response was that they must have him confused
with his brother Milton, whose career included the presidency of
Kansas State University, Pennsylvania State University, and Johns
Hopkins University. Although Columbia was not what Ike had in
mind, Milton advised him to accept, which he did in 1948. When
some heard that an Eisenhower had been named president, they
assumed that it was Milton. In fact, there was some controversy
over Eisenhower's appointment. A number of faculty bristled that
the position had not gone to an academic. A few showed outright

hostility not only to Ike but also to Mamie. A letter writer, identifying himself only as a male alumnus of Columbia, suggested that she go to a good hairdresser and get rid of her bangs. Another anonymous correspondent suggested that Mamie would look much nicer "if you didn't wear you hair like a six year old kid. . . . I can't understand why your husband doesn't notice it, because my husband certainly would. . . . I don't like to be so frank about a person's style of hair but I am telling you for your own good." Both letters were signed "A Friend." Jabs at Mamie's hairstyle were gnat stings compared with the rumors and nasty asides that Mamie endured in wartime Washington, and Mamie ignored whatever hostility she encountered at Columbia.[35]

Mamie was, in fact, happy at Columbia. Ike was home with her. John, who married Barbara Thompson in June 1947, was fairly close, teaching at West Point, and Mamie was a doting grandmother. Grandson David was born in 1948, and granddaughter Anne (Barbara Anne) was born while the Eisenhowers were at Columbia. Mamie's talents as a homemaker were allowed to express themselves as she renovated the president's mansion with the help of decorator Elisabeth Draper. Her charity work included the Manhattan Mission, where, working with David Rockefeller, money was raised for an after-school recreation center for underprivileged children. For Mamie, the activities of making a home and volunteering her time to worthwhile causes provided a sense of balance, and from her viewpoint, being the wife of a university president was not that different from life in the military. There was the same sort of entertaining, "only on a larger scale," and the deans down to nontenured professors created a hierarchy "like captains or majors or colonels in the Army."[36]

Mamie hosted teas for faculty wives and important donors to the university, but the Eisenhowers were still criticized for not using the president's home on Morningside Drive as a sort of all-purpose student/faculty club for university functions. Complaints to the contrary, the Eisenhowers entertained members of Columbia's academic community and important leaders from abroad, including Prime Minister Jawaharlal Nehru of India and his daughter, Indira Gandhi. The Eisenhowers also invited friends to dinners and for casual get-togethers. Mamie called one weekend with friends "a hilarious hen house party . . . just like the war days." Perle Mesta, who lived at the Wardman during the war, was there and taught everyone canasta. It became one of Mamie's favorite card games. As in earlier times, people were drawn to the warmth of the Eisenhowers' home. "Why you even made us believe that you were sad to see us go," wrote General Alfred Gruenther.[37]

In 1950, President Truman approached Ike about the North Atlantic Treaty Organization (NATO). Demobilization after the war had left Western Europe unprepared for defense against the Soviet Union, and there was strong resistance to rearming West Germany against the threat of the Red Army along what became known as the Iron Curtain. One thing that the Europeans seemed to agree upon was that Eisenhower could bring order to differing views and interests. In January 1951, Eisenhower went to Europe as the first Supreme Allied Commander, Europe (SACEUR). Columbia University trustees refused to accept his resignation, instead giving him a leave of absence. Ike and Mamie left for France, where the Eisenhowers were offered a choice of homes. Mamie chose a château outside Paris. The grounds were lovely, but the building, once occupied by Napoleon III and later by Louis Pasteur, required renovation. Several of the country's leading decorators were "loosed" on the structure. Mamie let them have their way, with the exception of the master bedroom. Using a postcard-size piece of plywood painted a shade of green, Mamie insisted on that color for the walls, as well as pink for the fabrics. This color scheme had been one constant in the Eisenhowers' many homes, providing a sense of permanency no matter where home happened to be.[38]

Meanwhile, the push to draft Eisenhower for political office continued. Several of Eisenhower's friends and supporters organized Citizens for Eisenhower, which, in turn, oversaw Ike Clubs nationally. Professional politicians wrote Ike or visited him in Paris. "Men of every kind and class . . . visited my headquarters during all of 1951," he later wrote. Mamie also heard from the public. On the one hand, there were the "don't let your husband make a fool of himself" sorts of letters. On the other, correspondents begged Mamie to persuade Ike to become a candidate. When the general returned to the United States for meetings related to NATO, Truman approached him and promised the Democratic nomination if Ike chose to run. Ike turned him down, just as he refused to make any commitment to the Republicans. In November 1951, Ike and Mamie flew to New York, where they met with Milton Eisenhower and Lucius Clay. The latter had retired from the army and was chairman of Continental Can in New York, spending a great deal of time with Citizens for Eisenhower. Clay was concerned about maintaining organization within Citizens for Eisenhower. Milton told his brother to consider whether he or Republican Robert Taft, an avowed non-interventionist, would be better for the country. Ike agreed that Taft was not the best choice, but he refused to involve himself in the political maneuvering that preceded primaries and political conventions. Still in uniform, Eisenhower could not declare himself a candidate without resigning from his position. The pressure was clearly building, and it continued when Ike and Mamie returned to Paris. To defuse some of the tension, Mamie added a touch of levity during a Christmas party hosted for friends. Packages of "I Like Ike" ties, beanies, and buttons had arrived with other holiday packages, and Mamie decided to put them to use. "While Ike was in the library we all put on the caps & buttons—when he came in his face turned red but he had to laugh because we looked so silly."[39]

Perhaps the turning point in his decision to run was seeing the two-hour film of the Citizens for Eisenhower rally held in Madison Square Garden in February 1952. Jacqueline Cochran, the famous aviator who headed the Women's Airforce Service Pilots during World War II, and her husband, Floyd Odum, a wealthy businessman-financier, were among the rally sponsors, and it was Cochran who flew the film to Paris. Ike and Mamie were moved by the scenes of thousands of people shouting, "We want Ike!" and waving "I Like Ike" banners. The film convinced Ike that people truly wanted him as a candidate.[40]

Ike continued to work vigorously as SACEUR, but he had decided, at least privately, to pursue the presidency. He discussed it with Mamie, knowing that being thrust into public life would demand a great deal of her. "He guessed no two people knew less about politics," Mamie later told a biographer, but she and Ike saw it as a duty to serve the country. Lucius Clay advised the general not to enter the campaign until June 1, and on that day he returned to the United States. "We looked around us, said good-bye to Europe, and turned toward home," he wrote. Mamie was leaving another home behind, but in a letter to Jacqueline Cochran, Mamie seemed to accept another change in her life with a shrug: "Oh! Well," she wrote.[41]

Three days after arriving in the States, Eisenhower gave his first nationally televised political speech, broadcast from a park in his Kansas hometown. Thanks to the rain that poured that day and his rather emotionless reading from a prepared text, the result was lackluster. Nevertheless, the Eisenhower campaign used the new medium of television to advantage. In filmed television spots Eisenhower answered posed questions, and it was not by accident that his "I shall go to Korea" speech was carried live on national television. Among the innovations were the "We Like Ike" campaign cartoons that Jacqueline Cochran convinced Walt Disney Productions to create. Although the Disney people had reservations, they soon realized the impact. "We had a great deal of fun in making the films," one of the filmmakers wrote Cochran, "and it was with pride that we viewed our work on television night after night." Although Ike appeared on live television, Mamie refused to address the viewing audience. She was perfectly happy to stand in the background, which led a longtime army acquaintance to write that her only "beef" with Ike's TV appearances was that Mamie was not in the spotlight often enough. "You are as pretty as a picture. . . . your clothes are out of this world and altogether, what is most important, you are the symbol of a happy home and as such are likely to linger in the memory of a great many people even longer than Ike's words, no matter how important and wise they may be."[42]

A few days after Eisenhower's speech in Abilene, campaign headquarters were set up at the Brown Palace Hotel in Denver. A more informal headquarters existed at the Doud home. Mamie's father had died in 1951, but Elivera still lived in Denver and was an enthusiastic supporter of her son-in-law. From Denver, Ike made a ten-day campaign trip through the Plains states, where his chief opponent for the Republican nomination, Robert A. Taft, had strong support. On July 5, Ike and Mamie arrived in Chicago for the Republican National Convention. Their suite and the Eisenhower campaign headquarters were at the Blackstone Hotel. Mamie knew that she would be under scrutiny, but she was no novice to being in the spotlight. Asked by a reporter if, as a "soldier's wife," she worried

Mamie and Ike greet supporters during a campaign stop in Ike's home state; at center is Kansas senator Frank Carlson. Dwight D. Eisenhower Library

about her son, John, who had received orders for Korea, Mamie responded that this was a "strange question to ask a mother." Soldier's wife or not, she was "still very much a mother." Thousands of women whose own sons and husbands were either in Korea or on their way felt an immediate connection to Mrs. Eisenhower.[43]

Mamie responded to the press with grace and often humor. When asked about Ike's hobby of painting, she told reporters that one portrait "started out as a tree," and when it came to her cooking skills, or the lack of them, she turned what might be considered a severe deficiency into a charming quirk. No, she was not a good cook. She readily admitted that, but the reporters might be interested in the wonderful way Ike broiled steaks over charcoal. Her good humor won admirers, including Hollywood gossip columnist Hedda Hopper, who took the podium at a luncheon for candidates' wives and heckled the contenders, except her own choice for president. Ike came in for his share of disparaging remarks, but Mamie kept smiling. Afterward, Hopper said, "That Mamie's quite a woman. I thought I'd make her sore, but instead she [later] asked my pardon for laughing and told me she loved the long-stemmed rose on my hat, even if it did bob up and down every time I nodded my head."[44]

This was the first national convention to be televised live, and Ike watched it, along with his brothers, from the Eisenhowers' suite at the Blackstone. As state delegates declared their choices, Mamie was in her room, suffering an allergic reaction to antibiotics prescribed for a painful tooth infection. When the nomination went to Eisenhower, he went to tell her. "It was, of course, a momentous thing," he wrote, "and both of us were somewhat overwhelmed by the future life our imagination pictured for us." Mamie later said, "Ike and I worked to win, but we counted on nothing." She was torn over the prospect of winning. She knew what a strain the presidency would be on her and Ike, but at the same time, there was a "wonderment" that it might happen. In the immediate hours and days after the nomination, congratulations poured in. Ruth Butcher's one-word telegram, "Speechless," might have easily described Mamie's own feelings. She wrote a family friend, "Chicago is already a dream to me—some of it hazy, but much of [it] exhilarating and inspiring." Mamie, now the wife of a presidential candidate, prepared for the fall campaign.[45]

The Republican candidate for president and his wife began a cross-country, whistle-stop campaign. The train was still considered the most effective way for a candidate to travel the country, meet the public, and make speeches. "Television was still in its childhood," explained one Eisenhower campaign strategist. "It had not yet become a substitute for one's own eyes and ears, and people still had a desire for personal contact with a candidate, even if it was at a distance." The campaign train, dubbed "Look Ahead, Neighbor," typically made from six to ten stops a day. At each one, Ike and Mamie appeared on the rear platform, where Ike spoke to the crowd and introduced Mamie. When the crowds first saw Mrs. Eisenhower, said a reporter, there was "a brilliant flash of communication." It was completely "illogical," but somehow Mamie invited "a feeling . . . [that] makes strangers feel her life must have been very much like their own." The fact that her life experiences were quite different from theirs seemed not to register at all. Mamie became "a veteran of the back platform, where she carried off her part beautifully." A *New York Times* political analyst declared Mrs. Eisenhower "worth at least

50 electoral votes." Ike, who was sometimes uncomfortable asking folks to vote for him, said, "She's a better campaigner than I am."[46]

The whistle-stop campaign covered more than 50,000 miles through forty-five states in eight weeks. On the train, Eisenhower sometimes met with local Republican leaders, and there were frequent meetings with campaign staff. Mamie did not attend these meetings, but when staff were invited to have lunch or dinner in the Eisenhowers' compartment, she did not shy away from offering opinions. "Some of Mamie's comments at the private meals were quite pointed," observed one strategist. "If she had a view of someone, she would express it in unadorned fashion." She had her own ideas. When Elivera Doud's cook asked Mamie to speak to her Black Republican Club, for example, Mamie agreed. The campaign managers were upset at not being consulted, and the clubs with white memberships were angry because they had been turned down. Mamie apologized to no one. She simply did what she thought was correct.[47]

At some stops, hundreds filed through the train to shake hands with the Eisenhowers. In big cities, the train stopped long enough for receptions, luncheons, and banquets. En route to these events, crowds were eager for a look at the candidate and his wife. Years later, while riding with Julie Nixon Eisenhower to her father's presidential inauguration, Mamie offered advice on responding to crowds with a wave. "Don't give them any of that prissy stuff," she said. "Give them a big wave. Really say hello." Mamie smiled and waved to those who came out to see her and Ike. She gave interviews on the train, in hotels, and at radio stations. She wrote a friend that she had done something she never thought possible—she made several back platform appearances alone. At the same time, she tried to keep up with correspondence to friends and well-wishers. Approximately 5,000 letters arrived each week, and Mamie personally replied to at least 75 each day. "I get up with letters, I go to bed with letters, I guess I'm what you'd call a well-lettered woman," she laughingly said. To one acquaintance, she wrote how grateful she and Ike were for their friends' hard work on their behalf: "That is what keeps Ike and I going on days when we are so tired."[48]

It was a grueling schedule. As the campaign wore on, Mamie came to dislike, to put it mildly, meeting and greeting the committee women and state officials who trooped onto the train at various stops. Although she would later say that she found the energy to push on when she saw the "hopeful" faces in the crowds, behind the scenes, the campaign was sometimes more difficult than she anticipated. When she began to hear the things that the opposition was saying about her husband, those closest to the campaign were aware that she "hit the ceiling" and tried to persuade Ike to withdraw his candidacy. She did not mind what people said about her, but their attacks on her husband, including accusations of his being anti-Semitic, were difficult to bear.[49]

"The mud-slinging that went on in the spring and early summer of 1952" between the Eisenhower and Taft camps, wrote John Eisenhower, "far transcended anything that occurred during the election campaign itself." Nevertheless, both political parties did what they could to smear the other in the race for the presidency. Rumors of Ike and Kay Summersby were circulated, and whispers resurfaced about Mamie's drinking. One of those blamed, unfairly or not, was Eleanor Roosevelt. The former first lady later told friends that President Eisenhower's refusal to reappoint her as a U.S. delegate to the United Nations rested on his belief that she helped spread the rumors. In what sounds like a contrived soap opera of intrigues, Eleanor believed that Perle Mesta, at that time U.S. ambassador to Luxembourg, told Ike that Eleanor was making broad innuendos. If Eleanor whispered into ears, she chose badly with Mesta. Although Perle was a Democrat and a Truman appointee, she was Mamie's friend. Two versions of the story have emerged. In one, Eleanor denied spreading gossip, particularly since both her father and brother died from drink. In the second version, Eleanor was said to have shrugged off her own family's questions by explaining that she had not *said* Mamie was drinking; she had only suggested it by asking *if* she was drinking. Admirers of Eleanor Roosevelt may find the whole affair unsettling, but she had a penchant for involving herself in partisan politics, and she passionately supported Adlai Stevenson. And, who said what is almost beside the point. The Eisenhower campaign could have quashed the rumors by simply releasing Mrs. Eisenhower's medical records and explaining Ménière's disease. The presidential candidates made public disclosures that year regarding their health, but asking the same sort of thing from a potential first lady was unheard of. Had it been suggested that the campaign make a public statement, Mamie probably would have balked. As she later told Barbara Walters in a television interview, she did not believe that you should tell your personal troubles to people. Mamie's sense of propriety made her balk at personal disclosures in a public forum.[50]

The campaign had considerable momentum when the *New York Post* ran a story that vice presidential candidate Richard Nixon had a "secret fund" of $18,000 given by a group of California millionaires. Other politicians accepted contributions, but the Democrats, saddled with their own corruption scandals, pounced on the story as a sign of underhanded dealings in the Republican camp. Some Eisenhower advisers wanted to drop Nixon from the ticket, but Ike agreed with the idea of Nixon taking his case to the American people via national television. The result was the famous "Checkers speech" in which Nixon asked that his daughters be allowed to keep their dog, Checkers, a gift from a contributor. The speech is also remembered for Pat Nixon seated off to one side while her husband told the viewing audience that his wife owned no fur coat, just "a respectable Republican cloth coat." The public response to Nixon was overwhelmingly positive, and there was no more discussion of his leaving the ticket.[51]

A few days after the speech, Eisenhower and Nixon appeared together at an outdoor rally in Wheeling, West Virginia. Mamie and Pat Nixon rode to the event together. The women barely knew each other, having only first met at the Republican convention, where, reportedly, Mamie's first words to Pat were, "You're the prettiest thing." On that evening in Wheeling, the two were subdued. Mamie broke the silence by saying, "I don't know why all this happened when we [the campaign] were getting along so well." From her point of view, Nixon had added another, and unneeded, burden on Ike. To Mamie's complaint, Pat snapped back that Mamie had no idea what the Nixons had just been through. Nothing more was said, but at the rally, Mamie draped her white fox fur over both their shoulders to ward off the cold. The image of the two women standing shoulder to shoulder was representative of a relationship that matured during the next eight years from the expediency of working together to one of mutual admiration.[52]

On election eve, Ike and Mamie returned by train to New York and cast their votes the next day. (Mamie was briefed beforehand on using a voting machine.) That evening, they joined friends at a suite

*Mamie was delighted when son John was given a brief leave
from Korea for Ike's inauguration.
Dwight D. Eisenhower Library*

in the Commodore Hotel to watch the election returns. Eisenhower received 55.1 percent of the popular vote. By the early hours of the next morning, the results were clear. Adlai Stevenson conceded the election at about 1:30 A.M., and the president-elect and his wife went to the hotel's ballroom to greet enthusiastic supporters. In the weeks that followed, Ike kept his campaign promise and went to Korea. Mamie visited Bess Truman for the traditional tour offered to the incoming first lady. The two had gotten to know one another when Ike was chief of staff and Mamie was invited to the White House to attend Bess Truman's Spanish classes. The classes were described as a way to promote "inter-American friendship." Mamie called them "hen parties." Just as Mamie maintained a friendship with Jean MacArthur when their husbands were often at odds in the Philippines, she did not let animosity between Ike and Harry Truman influence her friendship with Bess. Others might choose friends on the basis of politics or partisan convenience, but not Mamie.[53]

On inauguration day, January 20, 1953, Dwight David Eisenhower became the thirty-fourth president of the United States. The swearing-in ceremony was nationally televised. At his inauguration, Eisenhower did two things that no other president had done. He read a prayer of his own composition, and after the oath of office was administered, he kissed his wife for all to see. *Life* magazine captioned its photograph of the moment: "Presidential kiss is bestowed on Mamie as everybody in stands almost bursts with beaming."[54]

CHAPTER 3

BEING FIRST LADY
IN THE 1950S

On inauguration day 1953, the traditional parade followed the solemn swearing-in ceremony and Eisenhower's speech to the nation. No Republican had served in the White House since Herbert Hoover, and the GOP was determined to celebrate in a grand way. The parade, which was the largest up to that time, began to form at midday and did not end until almost seven that evening. Mamie gamely sat through the whole event. Ike stood. "I have never seen anything as gracious as the two of you seeing the parade through to the bitter end," Ruth Butcher later told Mamie. Watching the parade was an official duty of the president and first lady, but anyone observing Mamie would have noticed that her smiles and waves throughout the long day reflected a gift for conveying the impression of genuine enjoyment. Despite the cold, she later called the seemingly endless event "grand fun."[1]

During the campaign and then after Ike's election, reporters asked and ordinary citizens wondered what sort of first lady Mamie Eisenhower would be. The instant connection that Mrs. Eisenhower made with whistle-stop crowds created a feeling of familiarity. The public saw "Mrs. Average America . . . congenial suburban housewife . . . member of the garden club . . . fun-loving grandmother." She seemed to personify the conventional middle-class woman, despite experiences as a military wife that were anything but typical.

Ike and Mamie on the morning of the inaugural ceremonies.
Dwight D. Eisenhower Library

Commentators wondered how the various public perceptions of
Mrs. Eisenhower would translate into Mamie, the first lady. *Time*
magazine asked those who knew her. "Mamie will never be stuffy,"
one friend promised. She could rise to any occasion without becoming overly impressed with herself. "I saw her in Europe," said another acquaintance. "There was this King Haakon [of Norway], and
there was Mamie, talking with her hands, just as peppy as ever." A reporter who followed the presidential campaign for *Life* had his own

take on the new first lady: "She will have the highly commendable dignity of Bess Truman enlivened with a touch of Ethel Merman on the side." Shortly after the presidential election, *U.S. News & World Report* told its readers that Mrs. Eisenhower would not try to shape public opinion or policy as had Mrs. Roosevelt. Nor would she remain in the background as had Mrs. Truman. What Mrs. Eisenhower would or would not do was all fodder for speculation.[2]

As for Mamie, she needed no coaching or advice, no media or image consultants. Although she had met four of her predecessors in the previous twenty years and she regarded Edith Wilson and Bess Truman as friends, she did not plan to model herself after any particular first lady. She was going to be herself, and she stepped into the role with supreme confidence. As she later told an interviewer, she felt that both she and Ike were "better equipped" for the White House than some others would have been. Their military life had introduced them to unique experiences that took them to overseas postings and brought them in contact with foreign heads of state and dignitaries. Army life had taught them to adapt to their surroundings, although adaptation had sometimes been a difficult lesson for Mamie to learn. Ike's notoriety after World War II also brought limitations to their everyday lives, and they had learned to live with security precautions long before the Secret Service came into their lives. While they were in Paris, for example, anti-NATO protests made it necessary for the Eisenhowers to have bodyguards. Other modern presidential families usually took time to adjust to the restrictions that came with living in the White House, but these were not new to Mamie. "I have been forced to limit my going and coming for quite a few years," she said. She felt prepared to take on the role of first lady, although Mamie confided to Bella Hall, a friend from the days spent at Fort Myer, that once in the White House she sometimes missed being a "carefree individual" who could see her friends whenever she chose.[3]

On her first full day in the White House, Mamie Eisenhower visited with her daughter-in-law and son, whom Truman brought home from Korea for the inauguration. Mamie then attended to the most pressing mail, greeted 300 Republican women at a reception, and met with the Executive Mansion's chief usher on matters relating to the household. The White House over which she would preside had just seen a complete structural renovation and modernization during the Truman administration. In fact, following Bess Truman's tour of the White House after the election, Mamie wrote Perle Mesta that she "was much impressed by the results of the renovation." There was a new lower basement, a solarium, and a movie theater. The house was now air-conditioned, and the Eisenhower grandchildren would be the first to use the new playroom on the third floor. With the exception of first-floor rooms and the second-floor Lincoln and Rose bedrooms, the first lady could bring in whatever furniture and fabrics she wished to use on the second and third floors. For the family residence, she kept much of the furniture that was already there, but she added some of her own pieces. Among these were a desk that once belonged to Mamie's maternal grandmother and a spool bed that came from Ike's grandfather. As in their earlier homes, the Eisenhowers' bedroom was done in fabrics with shades of pink and that "certain shade of green" for the walls. Although there were separate bedrooms for the presidential couple, the pink and green bedroom was theirs. This, said one of the ushers, was "a novelty." Not within the memory of anyone working at the White House had the president and his wife shared the same bed.[4]

Although the White House was newly redone, its third floor was not completely finished. With only $375 in the White House account for decorating, Mamie improvised as she had done so many times before. She purchased parachute silk at Fort Myer, and the White House seamstress made draperies for the third-floor windows. As the family residence became home, it took on what one of her friends called "a 'Mamie look,'" which the friend added was "all to the good." Mamie would have liked to do more with the Executive Mansion, but the recent renovations left little money.[5]

Her desire to decorate solely for her taste was directed at the Eisenhowers' Gettysburg home. While at Columbia University, the Eisenhowers began to search for a place to live in retirement. They looked in Virginia and Connecticut. Well-known radio commentator Lowell Thomas suggested that the couple consider his area in New York State. The Eisenhowers were drawn to Gettysburg, Pennsylvania, however, and in 1950 they purchased the farm that was meant to be their home after Ike left Columbia. Although that retirement was deferred, Mamie was still determined to have a place that she and Ike actually owned. Her entire married life had been spent in apartments, military quarters, or homes that were essentially on loan. She loved the farm's location, with its trees and proximity to the historic Gettysburg Battlefield. And she loved the house, but when it turned out that most of the existing structure required almost complete demolition, she "made up her mind, come what may, to build her own." She hired interior designer Elisabeth Draper, who worked on refurbishing the president's home at Columbia University, and to the original house plans Mamie added such modern conveniences as central air-conditioning. The cost was more than $200,000.[6]

Since the couple's marriage, the farm and house were their first major purchase. The reported six-figure payment Ike received from selling the rights to his well-received *Crusade in Europe* helped substantially. Although the Eisenhowers' home was larger and more costly than the average one constructed during the 1950s—a typical one-story, three-bedroom home averaged about $15,000—the Eisenhowers were in step with the postwar building boom that saw more than 13 million new homes constructed between 1948 and 1958. Ike and Mamie, home builders and home owners, confirmed the American public's belief in and desire for home ownership.[7]

Mamie handled the financial demands of the Gettysburg property, and she carefully managed the White House accounts. The president's salary was $100,000 per year (about $55,000 after taxes). To this amount was added a $50,000 allowance for personal family expenses. From that, the Eisenhowers paid the salaries of any domestic help and White House staff who were not federal employees. This included Rosie Woods, who had been Mamie's personal maid since Fort Myer; John Moaney, an African American who had been Ike's orderly during the war and acted as his valet in the White House; and Moaney's wife, Delores, who was in charge of the family's living quarters at the White House. Out of the $50,000 allowance, the Eisenhowers also paid for personal phone calls, bills for personal laundry, clothing, and food for the family's meals and those of private guests. There was an additional allowance of $40,000 earmarked for paying the expenses for official travel and entertaining. Any costs above that amount were charged to the Eisenhowers. The well-organized Mamie oversaw the accounts, keeping the family's personal finances separate from those of the White House, often saying, "Don't run it on the Eagle [government]."[8]

While President Eisenhower set about balancing the national budget, Mamie kept the household accounts. Throughout the Eisenhowers' married life, Mamie handled the family finances, and there was no reason to change once Ike was elected. She was known for cost-cutting measures, and she was occasionally appalled that some people believed that she, as first lady, had unlimited resources. For the family's personal meals, she budgeted $100 a month. As cost-saving measures, she used vegetables grown at the Eisenhowers' Gettysburg farm, kept track of store advertisements for bargains, and insisted that dinner leftovers be used in the next day's lunch. "The cooks learned to turn out lots of casseroles and ground-meat dishes," similar to the fare served in the average American household. And, "woe to the chef" if the kitchen failed to use leftovers. Mamie kept track of what was consumed, and she knew what was in the pantry and freezer.[9]

Any discussions of Mamie Eisenhower's working days in the White House include the ubiquitous stories of her working from bed in the morning. She portrayed the routine as a small indulgent luxury that women should do for themselves whenever possible. There was more, however, to the morning routine than creature comforts. Mamie spent time in bed to conserve her energy and health. There were still episodes associated with Ménière's, and the rheumatic fever of her childhood had a long-term effect on her heart. She sometimes experienced shortness of breath, fatigue, and sudden palpitations that made her heart go "like a trip hammer." Probably the first evaluation and diagnosis by a cardiologist occurred in January 1946 at Walter Reed Army Hospital; in 1951 another cardiologist and one of Ike's consultants, Dr. Thomas W. Mattingly, examined Mamie. He recommended that she "continue to have a degree of restriction of her physical activities" and "avoid such instances where she will be unnecessarily hurried." So it was that Mamie worked from bed, and she sometimes allowed friends to visit with her. Newspaperman Cyrus Sulzberger, head of the *New York Times* foreign service and a friend from Eisenhower's NATO days, was received in Mamie's bedroom. "Mamie greeted me like a long-lost friend," he wrote. "She was sitting up in bed in a pink bedjacket.

She stretched out her arms and kissed me on both cheeks, sat me down beside her and we started to chat. . . . She loves the job of running the White House. She finds she can handle all the work."[10]

Much of that work began from bed. Before she had breakfast and began dealing with staff, she read the morning papers, noting sale advertisements for foodstuffs and other items that would be useful in the White House. When the head usher came in with her breakfast tray, they went over the menus for the day and details for any upcoming social events. The White House housekeeper and Mamie's secretary, Mary Jane McCaffree, followed him. Mamie dictated letters for two or three hours a day and, with McCaffree, went over arrangements for events planned for the day and who she would see. The appointments schedule provided Mrs. Eisenhower with background information on the visitors being greeted, if there was to be some sort of presentation, and if photographs would be taken. A typical afternoon, illustrated by her schedule for a week in February 1953, included accepting an elephant pin and earring set from members of a women's Republican club, greeting eight members of a Girl Scout troop that worked with children with cerebral palsy, accepting a box of Girl Scout cookies from another troop, meeting the winner of the National Cherry Pie Baking Contest, and posing for photographs with two women in charge of the membership drive for the Army-Navy League. Personal appearances of this sort were expected of first ladies. Eleanor Roosevelt's involvement was intermittent for the simple reason that she was frequently traveling out to meet people, rather than receiving them at the White House. Bess Truman made personal appearances "with groups who thought they could benefit from a photo with the First Lady," and Jacqueline Kennedy, who "was reluctant to spend a lot of time with women's groups," oftentimes found excuses to cancel. If Mamie's patience was taxed by these appearances, she never showed it. Instead, she gave the impression of thoroughly enjoying the photo sessions and the people she met.[11]

Public demands on her time coexisted with Mamie's insistence that she run the household. She did not simply leave the details to staff. Of her approach, J. B. West, who advanced from usher to head usher during the Eisenhower years, said: "The White House was easier to operate during Mrs. Eisenhower's regime. She knew her own mind and we [the staff] appreciated it. . . . As the wife of a career army officer, she understood the hierarchy of a large establishment, the division of responsibilities, and how to direct a staff. She knew exactly what she wanted, every moment, and exactly how it should be done . . . as if it were she who had been the five-star general. She established her White House command immediately."[12]

The staff quickly learned that, although Mrs. Eisenhower "appeared fragile and feminine," she could give orders "staccato crisp," and that her rules were to be followed. An early lesson came two weeks after the Eisenhowers moved into the White House. Mamie was shown a menu for one of Ike's famous stag luncheons, which he described as a chance to enjoy good company while gaining "information and intelligent opinion" from leaders in business, government, labor, the arts, and education. On this particular menu was the notation, "Approved DDE." Mamie shook her head, informing the head usher that "in the future all menus are to be approved by *me* and not by anybody else!" Mrs. Eisenhower insisted on supervising everything, from the menus to the flowers chosen for table arrangements. She also expected precise forms of address for the staff. Whereas the chief usher was always to be addressed as "Mr.," the servants were to be called by their first names. Mrs. Eisenhower was known for using the white-glove treatment to check for dust, and she insisted on frequent vacuuming to eliminate foot marks on carpets, particularly in the public areas. When members of the press were allowed in to view the decorations before a state dinner, Mary Jane McCaffree invariably cautioned them "not to step on the rug."[13]

"It always seemed to us [staff]," said West, "that Mrs. Eisenhower's 'taut ship' approach to directing activities in the Executive Mansion only reflected the way the General ran the Presidency." Mamie was a perfectionist. When someone was careless, she "could be imperious," said West. And, with Ike's personal secretary, Ann Whitman, she was correct and formal, belying the tension between the two women. Whitman was working as a secretary in the New York office of Crusade for Freedom when she was recruited for Ike's 1952 presidential campaign. She was one of several secretaries traveling on the campaign train, but after she began to act as Ike's personal secretary, she suspected that Mamie wanted her removed. "Knowing Mrs. E's power," Whitman wrote her husband, "I'm

pretty sure I'm out." She stayed, but the frosty relationship remained. Whitman later said that Mamie resented her because the
first lady was not "a participant in Eisenhower's professional life,"
but John Eisenhower had another opinion. "Mother liked to think
that she ran the home," he said. "But Ann would plead exigency to
avoid telling Mamie what was going on. . . . She did nothing to spare
Mother's feelings." Mamie had no other choice than to develop a
functional working relationship with Whitman and once included
her on the guest list for a state dinner that Whitman called "a sort of
starry-eyed wonder."[14]

As for the White House staff under her direction, it was generally
agreed that Mrs. Eisenhower was easy to work for because everyone
knew exactly what was expected. Mamie's manner was softened by
the genuine interest she took in everyone associated with the White
House. She asked after them and their families not in a "perfunctory
manner" but because she wanted to know. She let them in on her
life, and she "took an interest in everything in ours." When there was
a new baby in someone's family, Mamie sent a gift, either a monogrammed baby spoon or cup. It made no difference what job the
child's parent did at the White House. Among the recipients, for example, were the children of Secret Service agents, ushers, the man
who ran the movies in the White House theater, and a magician who
entertained at granddaughter Anne's birthday party.[15]

The first lady had definite ideas about how the White House
should function. She stopped the president's staff and White House
Social Office employees from using the mansion as a quick way to
get back and forth between the East Wing and West Wing. The mansion was not a "passageway," she told them, and no one from the
West Wing staff was allowed into the family residence without the
first lady's permission. As much as possible, Mamie was determined
to maintain a line between home and work. The family residence
was a refuge in which Ike could relax. This was not intended as a
slight to the uninvited. It was the way in which they compartmentalized their lives. Still, there were hurt feelings. Secretary of State
John Foster Dulles complained to Walter Trohan of the *Chicago
Tribune* that he was never invited to the family residence for dinner, although he worked with Ike many times until the dinner
hour. Reportedly, Vice President Nixon also complained of never

being invited. His wife, however, was. Only two days after the 1953 inauguration, Mamie took Pat to the residence. "She was most friendly," Mrs. Nixon wrote to longtime friend Helene Drown. "[She] took me up to her living quarters . . . and showed me all the rooms." The rules for the West Wing contingent did not apply to Mrs. Nixon, who Mamie was still getting to know at this early juncture of the Eisenhower administration and who would be a valued ally in carrying out official duties.[16]

Conversely, Mrs. Eisenhower did not go to the West Wing to simply visit, and certainly there were no situations in which Mamie sat in while policy was discussed. In the eight years of living in the White House, she went to Ike's office only four times, "and I was invited each time." This was a result of the Eisenhowers' formula for keeping home and work separate, as well as a holdover from army life. She later told an interviewer: "A wife never went near headquarters. You never went to his place of operation."[17]

This did not mean that Mamie was oblivious to the issues of the day or had no opinions. When Eisenhower was president-elect, she sat in with him during at least two CIA briefings that dealt with Korea. While her concern was with John, who was serving there, one of the CIA officers came away with the impression that she was "much more political than Ike." She was a good judge of people, and Ike respected her opinions. Nonetheless, Mamie Eisenhower did not see herself in the mold of activist Eleanor Roosevelt, serving as "eyes and ears" for her husband. Nor would she have used the first lady position, as did Rosalynn Carter and Hillary Clinton, to define the first lady's role as an equal partner in shaping policy.[18]

Mamie Eisenhower once said that the voters elected her husband, not her. Her responsibilities lay in the traditional realm of successfully managing a household, albeit a very large one. The approach was a good fit for the 1950s and the decade's culture of domesticity, but the issue of domesticity was more complex than the simple perception that after World War II, women stayed home to be wives and mothers. Betty Friedan's book *The Feminine Mystique* made a strong case for arguing that social pressures forced women to stay home, although Friedan and others looked at the fifties through the lens of their own experiences. They were thinking of educated middle- and upper-class white women, not the less educated or less affluent.

Their voices were not those of African American women or low-income whites who, studies showed, would have preferred to move out of the labor force and be full-time wives and mothers. The reality for America's women was a spectrum of circumstances that included not only the question of if women worked outside the home, but why.[19]

Despite cultural images of domesticity, particularly those portrayed in the popular press and on television, the number of women in the American workforce steadily increased during the decade. By 1958, there were 22 million working women in the United States. Of that number, more than 16 million were, or had been, married, and more than 7 million had children under the age of eighteen. Studies, including one in 1956, showed that while a small proportion of women with very young children worked outside the home, "older married women, once a small minority among women workers, are now the largest group." Financial considerations were a major factor in a woman's decision to seek full- or part-time employment. Personal satisfaction, earning money to purchase "extras" for the home, and more career options also played a part in the decision to work outside the home or pursue nondomestic interests. Mamie saw this within her own circle of military women when Marjory Ridgway, wife of incoming army chief of staff Matthew Ridgway, let it be known in 1953 that she would not be accepting many social invitations from Washington hostesses—already an accomplished artist, she planned to seriously study painting with a professional instructor.[20]

The mass culture of the decade was filled with contradictory messages and differing experiences. A case in point was the role of women in politics. Not only were women encouraged to participate as voters and campaign volunteers, but several women served in Congress or held key positions in the Eisenhower administration and/or government agencies. Among those in Congress were Representatives Frances P. Bolton (R-OH) and Marguerite Stitt Church (R-IL), as well as Senator Margaret Chase Smith (R-ME). Counted in the number of women serving in government agencies was Katherine Howard; onetime secretary for the National Republican Committee, she became an administrator in the office of Federal Civil Defense. And there was Oveta Culp Hobby, who headed the

WACs during World War II and then became a very visible example of women's achievements in government service during Eisenhower's first term. She was the first secretary of the new agency, Health, Education, and Welfare, and only the second female cabinet member in U.S. history.[21]

During the Eisenhower administration, 175 women held high-level federal posts. Among them were Ike's appointments of Frances E. Willis as ambassador to Switzerland, former congresswoman Clare Boothe Luce as ambassador to Italy, and Mary Pillsbury Lord as U.S. representative to the United Nations Human Rights Commission and then U.S. delegate to the U.N. Assembly. Perhaps it was because Ike recognized the contributions women made during World War II, both on the home front and in the military, that he elevated women to important positions. In 1956 he also wholeheartedly supported Jacqueline Cochran's bid for a congressional seat. When she lost, Ike telegraphed her: "Your loss is to me a personal one for I know so well what fine work you would have done in Congress." And, what did Mamie, the consummate homemaker, think of women working outside the home? "The decision is completely up to them," she told an interviewer. "If a woman wants to express herself outside the home or if the budget needs the outside income for extra luxuries, only the woman herself can make the decision." Mamie was not blindly tied to traditional expectations for women's roles. She was realistic. As a young woman, she had seen women's choices expand during the New Woman repudiation of Victorian traditions, and she believed that women could decide their own course. That she chose to emphasize the role of wife and mother did not, in her eyes, diminish the choices made by other women.[22]

During the 1996 Mamie Doud Eisenhower Centennial hosted at the Eisenhower Presidential Library, Mary Jane McCaffree, Mamie's personal secretary, was asked to discuss the first lady's relationship with the press. McCaffree laughed and replied, "She didn't have any relationship with the press." McCaffree was referring to the lack of press conferences. Unlike Eleanor Roosevelt, who held more than 300 press conferences in twelve years, Mamie Eisenhower had only one during the eight years she was in the White House. Held on

March 11, 1953, that conference began on a light note. When Mamie welcomed the reporters with "Good morning," they responded "Good morning, teacher." After a bit of laughter, Mamie told the reporters, "That's just what I feel like." The conference itself was unremarkably ordinary. Mamie recited the list of official events for the upcoming week and took questions that ranged from what furniture she had brought to the White House to when she had last driven a car. (The answer was 1936.) The conference was, however, notable for an innovation. Mrs. Roosevelt limited her press conferences to women correspondents. Mamie let the men in because, said a reporter, "Mrs. Eisenhower obviously believes in equal rights for men . . . and the men reporters, no fools, outnumbered the women."[23]

One female reporter later wrote of the press conference:

Mamie—whoever thinks of her as Mrs. Eisenhower—was such an unqualified success at her first news conference last week that even the opposition press, which hasn't said a good word yet for her husband or his administration, whipped out superlatives and cooed over the First Lady. . . . It has been obvious for a long time that all Mamie Eisenhower has to do to sell herself to press or public is just to be herself, which she inevitably is. She combines the qualities the American public has always cottoned to at all times: common sense, good taste, kindly manners, unpretentiousness and warm friendliness.[24]

Mamie was, in fact, well practiced in the art of meeting reporters. She had been plunged into the media world during the war years, and she became more adept during the campaign. Her good reviews from the Washington crowd did not inspire her, however, to continue the press conferences. It was McCaffree who met with reporters on a weekly basis. She issued statements concerning the social calendar, official events, and sometimes what Mrs. Eisenhower would be wearing. Added to the briefings were press releases that often described in detail the first lady's clothing for special occasions.

If reporters hoped for additional information, they were asked to submit their questions in writing. This applied not only to the White House press corps but to all print media. It was rather easy, for example, to respond to a questionnaire submitted by a writer for the *Progressive Farmer* who evidently clung to the belief that

Mrs. Eisenhower was too modest to brag about her cooking skills and wanted details. Had the first lady done any cooking in the White House? Had she prepared any recipes during the past two years? The answer to both was "no." More problematic were questionnaires that asked more complex questions. Murray Snyder, assistant White House press secretary, looked over the questions submitted in 1955 by a writer for *Look* magazine and declared them an "excellent" basis for "a fine magazine piece." Nevertheless, he strongly advised against answering them. "Several of the major questions," he told McCaffree, "impinge on the question of whether the President will run again in 1956." This particular questionnaire also raised the difficulty of granting one writer access to information that had not been provided to all correspondents. While Mamie was still at Columbia University, she began a policy of granting no interviews that gave one writer more access than another. With the exception of Dorothy Brandon, a correspondent for the *New York Herald Tribune* who was given access to write Mamie's biography soon after Eisenhower's election, the no-favoritism policy continued during the White House years. It made no difference who asked for an interview or submitted questions. A high school girl describing herself as "a star reporter" on the school paper was gently refused an exclusive interview, just as the *Saturday Evening Post* was turned down when it proposed that Mamie write an autobiographical piece for publication.[25]

Reporters and journalists accepted the limitations with fairly good humor because Mamie did not break the no-favoritism policy. During her years in the White House, the first lady generally received good press from magazine and newspaper writers. When a black-owned newspaper in Washington, D.C., printed a "friendly article" on Mamie, Maxwell Rabb, who had the unprecedented job of being in charge of minority affairs, called it "wonderful"—not only because the paper was owned and operated by African Americans but because the paper was committed to policies of the Democratic Party. Mamie could make people forget partisanship. And, although she showed no interest in holding additional press conferences, she found other ways to court the press. Newswomen were asked to tea, and Mamie was the first to invite women of the press to a formal White House luncheon, replete with china and carefully selected table decorations. That men were not included was indicative of the time period. News organizations considered covering the first lady a woman's job. Invitations to these White House functions were not restrictive. Any accredited newswoman, including Alice A. Dunnigan from the Association of the Negro Press, was invited. Recalled one of the journalists who attended Mamie's social occasions for newswomen: "Shaking hands warmly with all, the First Lady stopped often to chat, with surprising memory for names and faces. Such talents in a President's wife, I reflected, may not make headlines. But certainly they increase the effectiveness of a Nation's leader."[26]

Mrs. Eisenhower's personal secretary, Mary Jane McCaffree, was also social secretary and press secretary. McCaffree would later tell Letitia "Tish" Baldrige, incoming social secretary for Jacqueline Kennedy, that first ladies needed a larger support staff to handle the mail, as well as the demands of social and press obligations. McCaffree spoke from firsthand experience, but despite the daunting job, she handled the three jobs with great efficiency. She had, in fact, an established career as an executive secretary, beginning in 1937, when she was secretary to the general manager of the New York World's Fair and then secretary to the fair's vice president in charge of protocol. By 1952, when McCaffree began her association with Mrs. Eisenhower, she also had been a personal secretary for two corporate presidents and an office manager for Citizens for Eisenhower, while her husband, Dr. Floyd E. McCaffree, was director of research for the Republican National Committee.[27]

In dealing with the press, McCaffree was more than competent, but when she had questions, she turned to James Hagerty, Eisenhower's press secretary and the man White House reporter James Deakin credited with creating the role of the modern press secretary. Especially in the early days of the administration, Hagerty offered McCaffree his expertise in dealing with some of the prickly problems that were bound to appear. When, for example, a reporter with White House credentials asked for access to Mamie, McCaffree checked with Hagerty. He responded that this particular reporter was "a 'bad' girl" who should be avoided. What exactly warranted this response was not explained in Hagerty's memo, but McCaffree heeded the advice. In other instances, particularly those that could reflect upon both Eisenhowers, Hagerty dealt with the situation. On one occasion, *Publisher's Weekly* announced that Victor Lasky was "popping in and out of the White House" in preparation of writing a first lady biography that would be serialized in a popular magazine. Since the White House was careful to avoid the image of playing favorites, Hagerty had "a heart to heart talk" with the would-be biographer. "Believe me," the press secretary later told McCaffree, "he is a much chastened gentlemen" who promised to put an end to the rumors. Columnist Drew Pearson was more difficult, although Hagerty made the effort. Just a few months after the Eisenhowers were in the White House, Pearson wrote that psychic Jeanne Dixon was visiting the Executive Mansion, giving Ike and Mamie up-to-date readings on their futures. It was a ludicrous claim, and Hagerty wrote as much to Pearson. The truth was that the Eisenhowers did not know Dixon; in fact, they probably had never heard of her before Pearson's column appeared.[28]

Pearson was one of the best-known columnists of his time, part investigative reporter and part gossip. His favorite targets were politicians and members of presidential administrations. Throughout the Eisenhower presidency, Pearson periodically criticized Ike and Mamie, although Pearson had once been an Ike supporter. Pearson first brought Eisenhower's name before the American public in 1941 when he praised Colonel Eisenhower's abilities during the Louisiana Maneuvers. Later, when Ike was at NATO, Pearson traveled to Europe to tell Ike that he believed the Taft people were buying votes in the South prior to the Republican convention. Pearson became disenchanted, however, believing that Eisenhower was easily influenced and impressed by men of wealth. He skewed the president on many occasions, and he singled out Mamie's trips to Elizabeth Arden's Maine Chance spa in Arizona during the president's second term. Pearson complained that taxpayer dollars were misused when Ike rerouted the president's plane to pick her up in Phoenix. The next year, Mamie traveled by train, but Pearson was not to be put off. In what he snidely called "Operation Mamie," Pearson accused her of violating the railroad law that made it illegal for public officials to accept free transportation. That Mamie was not technically a public official seemed not to matter, and Pearson continued to lambaste Mamie's yearly trips to the spa. An exasperated Mamie wrote

Arden, "We no longer pay attention to the false accusations appearing in newspapers."[29]

Pearson not only complained of Mamie's trips to Maine Chance but took swipes at her and her beloved Gettysburg home. The Eisenhowers used union labor on the project, but as the house neared completion, Mamie paid the expenses of White House carpenters and electricians to do some of the work, and she employed the gardener from Camp David during his off-duty hours. Pearson, however, intimated that the Eisenhowers had not purchased the Gettysburg farm with their own money. It was paid for by friends, he said. To that rumor, he added that the Eisenhowers avoided paying bills for follow-up improvements. Mamie later responded to the allegations by saying, "Ike and myself paid for every brick."[30]

It was true that the Eisenhowers received gifts for the farm and house. Ordinary citizens sent flower bulbs, packets of vegetable seeds, and various other items. Friends and supporters sent gifts. Jacqueline Cochran and her husband, for example, gave Ike an Angus cow. The Republican National Committees of the States and Territories sent fifty evergreen trees, and the White House staff surprised the Eisenhowers with a nineteenth-century mantel that once graced the East Room of the Executive Mansion. The gift was misrepresented by Pearson, who failed to note that the item was sold at auction by President Arthur in 1882 and then resurfaced in the hands of a private owner in the 1950s. The staff purchased it after the White House Fine Arts Commission decided not to restore it to the Executive Mansion. "We felt that in giving this gift . . . that the mantel was getting as close to the White House as possible—and into the home of a First Family who will cherish it always," explained McCaffree. Despite columnists such as Pearson, Mamie generally enjoyed good press and good relations with the media while first lady. Even when she made a misstep, as she did when it became known that the Eisenhowers paid $385 for a fur coat that retailed at $1,800, the criticism was short-lived after the press learned that Mrs. Eisenhower originally refused the coat when it was offered as a gift.[31]

James Hagerty's guidelines for White House press relations were passed on to John and Barbara Eisenhower. Although they generally adhered to a policy of refusing interviews, a few exceptions were made. Both, for instance, agreed to stories for *This Week: The National Sunday Magazine*. Barbara Eisenhower shared her ideas on having a good relationship with one's mother-in-law. The subject was probably on the minds of thousands of young wives, and the Barbara-Mamie relationship was one that many would envy. "I can tell you from experience that it's fun to have a daughter-in-law you love," the first lady wrote a friend whose son recently became engaged. For the same magazine, John talked about Ike as a father, including the things they had done together when John was a boy. The magazine piece was a good adjunct to the mounds of articles that were being published in the 1950s on motherhood, and it nicely corresponded with a national survey that showed men preferred being a husband and father to living the life of a "carefree" bachelor. Far less acceptable to the Eisenhowers were requests that came from people hoping to use the Eisenhower name for some sort of endorsement. One advertiser, for example, wanted to pair Barbara's name with its product. She let James Hagerty deal with the request and the correctly worded refusal. Just as often, however, the requests were for the couple's children to be photographed or serve as the focus of a magazine piece.[32]

In the years following the Eisenhower administration, numerous writers have said a great deal about America's fascination with and interest in the Kennedys because they were a "young" family. There is no doubt that this is true, but during the 1950s, President and Mrs. Eisenhower's grandchildren presented much the same image. "It is the first time in many years that young children have been in the White House," wrote an editor for *Women's Wear Daily*, who hoped that Barbara Eisenhower would allow an interview. The children were, trumpeted the editor, no different from the young British royals Princess Anne and Prince Charles, and, like it or not, the Eisenhower children were "public domain."[33]

As the grandchildren of General Eisenhower and then President Eisenhower, the children were photographed and written about from the time they were born. Shortly after the oldest grandchild, David, was born in 1948, *Parents* magazine invited its readers to "Meet Baby Ike," and while Eisenhower was president, a newspaper dubbed young David "First Boy." David's younger siblings Anne (born in 1949), Susan (born in 1951), and Mary Jean (born in 1955)

The Eisenhowers' granchildren, pictured here at the Gettysburg farm,
brought an image of youth to the White House,
from left to right are Anne, Mamie, Susan, Ike, and David.
National Park Service Photograph by Abbie Rowe, Dwight D. Eisenhower Library

were, along with David, photographed with their parents and grandparents at the White House. There were also photo stories of family outings at Camp David, Gettysburg, and Augusta National Golf Club. As doting grandparents, Ike and Mamie were happy to show off their grandchildren. John and Barbara were much more cautious, believing that "excessive publicity and attention" could easily spoil the children. For a period of time, John said, he and Barbara were perhaps more strict than they otherwise might have been. Nonetheless, they felt it necessary "in an effort to combat the artificial adulation" showered on the children by the press. America, however, was in the midst of a baby boom (between 1946 and 1960, 59.4 million children were born in the United States), and the Eisenhower grandchildren were attractive symbols of this generation. Young couples felt an affinity with John and Barbara Eisenhower, and older couples identified with President and Mrs. Eisenhower as grandparents. The children were certainly good copy for magazines and newspapers looking for ways to attract all those readers who had young children in the family.[34]

Adding to the youthful impression of the Eisenhower White House was Mamie herself. Dorothy Brandon first interviewed Mrs. Eisenhower at the Doud home in Denver while covering the 1952 campaign for the *New York Herald Tribune.* "It was impossible to believe that in a matter of months," wrote Brandon, "she would be fifty-six. Entirely without make-up except for lipstick, she could easily have cheated the calendar by two decades." Reporters and friends frequently commented that Mrs. Eisenhower looked younger than her years. Fashion designer Arnold Scaasi recalled that when he met Mamie, he was unprepared for "how pretty she was." Photographs did not do justice to her "exquisite coloring, her wonderful skin." The same response came years later, in 1966, when a writer for *McCall's* interviewed Mamie on her seventieth birthday. Her looks, wrote Vivian Cadden, "can only be described as astonishing. . . . [they] are extraordinary for a woman of her age." Mamie enhanced her image of a young grandmother in the White House by refusing to wear what she called "old lady clothes." At Brandon's first meeting with Mrs. Eisenhower in Denver, Mamie was wearing a sundress and sandals. In the White House, Mamie continued to follow her own style. Molly Parnis, a dress designer who catered to the elite of Washington and New York, observed that "Mrs. Eisenhower brings a new viewpoint on clothes to the White House. She's proving that a grandmother needn't be an old lady . . . she's making maturity glamorous."[35]

As a child, Mamie Eisenhower was taught that appearances mattered in both behavior and personal grooming. Her experiences as a military wife only reinforced the importance of appearances. In the letters she wrote to her parents over three decades, she sometimes remarked on a purchase or noted how she looked in a particular ensemble. In one instance, from 1929 in Paris, she wrote that she had spent 400 francs for a pair of shoes, but the expense was worth it. "I felt I looked smarter than any time since I'd been in Paris." Quite often, Mamie also remarked on son John's wardrobe. In a 1930 letter, for example, she wrote that eight-year-old John had just come into the room as she was writing—"he is wearing Palm Beach shorts."

Clothes and accessories were important to Mamie. She liked having them, and she enjoyed what she considered to be the therapeutic value of buying something new, not only for herself but also for others. Among her gifts to daughter-in-law Barbara was an evening gown from a Paris designer, and to her longtime employee Delores Moaney went a mink jacket. What Mamie chose to wear was an outward expression of the person and a personal statement of style. She was very conscious of the public impression she made.[36]

Mamie's style first received good reviews while she was on the campaign trail. Her "simple little suits or dresses [were] of good lines and flattering cut . . . her hats were right and her gloves spotless." When Ike was elected, America's fashion industry was delighted to see Mamie Eisenhower in the White House. "It occurs to me you may have no notion how happy the women in the country are, that finally we shall have a woman in the White House who is fashion-aware," wrote syndicated columnist Alice Hughes. "Both Mrs. Truman and Mrs. Roosevelt are fine human beings," continued Hughes, "but fashion was not forthcoming from them."[37]

The fashion industry hoped that Mamie's sense of style would give it a lift. Wartime shortages were a memory, replaced by a booming culture of consumerism, but the industry had its problems. The years of doing without during World War II had allowed a more casual attitude to creep into the popular culture. This was particularly noticeable among younger women. Fewer were wearing hats and gloves, except perhaps to church or some special function. Milliners were slowly losing their clientele, as were glove makers. More women, especially suburban housewives, were wearing slacks as leisure wear and for entertaining at home; teenage girls happily wore dungarees in public. Designers interested in high chic and manufacturers trying to anticipate middle-class tastes attempted to make sense of it all and find a way to tap into these changes. At the high end of the industry, American designers found it difficult to compete with the mystique of Paris fashion houses. No first lady could magically correct the industry's troubles, but a stylish one wielded considerable influence. Mamie seemed capable of doing just that. Even before the 1953 inauguration, the *New York Times* reported "a new spirit of optimism" among American clothing manufacturers and the buyers who decided what their stores would carry. "First reports," said the *Times,* "show a solid increase in orders for spring merchandise throughout the country."[38]

One of Mamie's first official fashion statements was her inaugural gown. Fashion experts and the press speculated beforehand on everything from who would design it to the probable color. Finally, the details were released, leading the *New York Herald Tribune* to observe that "after weeks of enough rumor and intrigue for a historical novel, the news has finally leaked out that Mrs. Eisenhower will dance in a Nettie Rosenstein gown at the inaugural ball." The peau de soie gown was "Renoir pink," studded with 2,000 rhinestones in varying shades of the same color. The inaugural gown set the stage for what the Textile Color Institute called "First Lady Pink" and popular culture dubbed "Mamie Pink." Although pink was not a dominant color in her wardrobe of dresses and suits, it became inseparable from the image of the first lady. She used pink extensively in decorating. In the Gettysburg home, her entire bathroom was pink—down to the cotton balls—and she used it when renovating the quarters at Camp David. Whether true or not, it was said that the White House staff became so accustomed to pink that when an employee was sent out to buy flannel for mop covers, he returned with pink flannel, explaining "everything else around here is pink, so we may as well have pink mops."[39]

Pink became a color associated with the 1950s. A paint company brought out "First Lady Pink" for home decorating. The color was seen in kitchen and bathroom tiles. Manufacturers produced pink appliances. Any modern American home could have a pink stove, refrigerator, ice crusher, or blender. The color was used for dinner sets and cookware. One company introduced a line of enameled pots and pans in "Fabulous Pink." Elvis had a pink and white Cadillac, and other car manufacturers used pink in two-tone combinations. And, when Mamie chose to wear the color, the result was memorable. Julie Nixon Eisenhower recalled the Nixon family's first visit with the Eisenhowers in California after the couple left the White House: "Toward the end of our tour [of fashionable Palm Springs], the former First Lady suggested we stop for ice cream. Mamie, in a hot-pink dress and matching short cashmere sweater, slightly tottering on her two-inch spike-heeled pink pumps, led the way into a drugstore."[40]

While Ike was at NATO, Mamie attended fashion shows in Paris and visited well-known design houses. She confided to a friend that "after being very penny-wise, last week I became pound-foolish and purchased two Paris gowns." Clothes and accessories from Paris designers were an exception in Mamie's wardrobe, however. As first lady, she wore clothes created by several American designers. Nettie Rosenstein, who designed the first inaugural gown, also designed the second. (Rather than pink, that gown was "citron-colored lace over matching taffeta.") Other designers were Hattie Carnegie; the designer Irene, who not only sold clothes under her own label but was under contract with Metro-Goldwyn-Mayer as a costume designer; and Arnold Scaasi, who created many of the gowns Mrs. Eisenhower wore to state dinners. Scaasi would later design clothes for Jacqueline Kennedy, Lady Bird Johnson, Barbara Bush, and Hillary Clinton. One of Mamie's favorite designers was Molly Parnis, who dressed other first ladies, including Pat Nixon. In the 1950s, Parnis was known for her full-skirted shirtwaist dresses and suits, and she conscientiously chose fabrics and designs that appealed to Mamie. "I hope she enjoys them as much as I enjoy making them," the designer wrote Mamie's secretary. For hats, Sally Victor was a perennial choice. Some of Victor's designs were created around the pillbox look, but unlike the unadorned pillbox later popularized by Jacqueline Kennedy, Mamie's were decorated with flowers or ribbon or braid.[41]

Mamie sometimes accepted gifts of costume jewelry, perfume, or bed jackets from designers, but she drew the line when they offered gifts of dresses, suits, and evening gowns. She insisted on paying, although designers, anxious to work within the first lady's budget in order to have her wear their clothes, did not charge full cost. As the incident with the $1,800 fur coat illustrated, Mamie did not necessarily pay retail prices. Her style put her on the best-dressed list, but she was no fashion snob. She was just as likely to buy a hat by mail order or purchase something off the rack from a department store. Department stores, whether they were upscale Neiman Marcus or middle-of-the-line J. C. Penney, benefited from the first lady's egalitarian attitude.[42]

Mamie accepted that the fashion world, and women around America, watched what she wore, but she had the self-confidence to refuse styles and faddish trends that she felt were unflattering. The long,

Hats were an expected fashion accessory during the 1950s. Mamie and Pat Nixon
(left) are shown at a 1954 Heart Fund charity event.
Dwight D. Eisenhower Presidential Library

pencil-thin silhouette look of the 1950s was not for her. Fads like the "sack" dress were ignored. When Dior raised hemlines in 1953, reporters, including Helen Thomas of United Press, hurried to find out if the first lady would follow the trend. She would not. She was comfortable with her current hemline. Fashions changed from one year to the next, and Mamie, like other women, disliked some of the "new" looks offered for a fashion season. Preparing for the 1956 Republican National Convention, Mamie confided to a friend that hats were a problem. The new styles were "hideous and most unbecoming."[43]

When Mamie disliked something, she would not wear it, and she ignored those fashion critics who voiced dismay over her dyed-to-match shoes, her "trademark" tinted gloves, and her love for charm bracelets. (Her favorite bracelet of "Ike" charms included a helmet, tank, five stars to denote five-star general, and a map of Africa symbolic of Ike's first World War II victory.) By ignoring these criticisms and personalizing her style, Mamie Eisenhower showed women that it was not necessary to follow every fashion dictate. And when she

At a 1956 Republican picnic held at the Gettysburg farm, Ike, along with
Vice-President and Mrs. Richard Nixon, admire the Dorothy Draper fabric
design of Mamie's dress. Scenes depicted Ike and Mamie's childhood homes
and the White House. United Press Photo

showed up at a Washington reception wearing a Molly Parnis dress almost identical to one being worn by another guest, the designer responded that this "is what makes this country a great democracy." The styles worn by the first lady were accessible to other American women.[44]

Mamie did not wear just anything that designers suggested, but there were some considerations that could not be overlooked. She quickly learned this in September 1953, when the White House let it be known that the first lady was planning to "wear last season's clothes." Mamie's "army training" and limited military pay had conditioned her to carefully select classic styles that outlasted a season's fashion fads. As much as she loved nice things, there was not always money to spend. When she was an army wife, there were numerous instances when clothes were reworked, with Mamie proud of the results. Writing to her parents during the 1930s, for instance, she told of admitting to friends that the black velvet dress they were "crazy about" was four years old and made over. She expected to continue this way of doing things as first lady. Designers were aghast. "We had a hard time convincing her that she couldn't wear two-year-old dresses," said Mollie Parnis. "It would be bad for our industry." Mamie relented.[45]

She would not relent, however, when it came to her hairstyle. When exactly she became "bobbed and banged" she later could not recall, but she was sure that her hair was first cut short for comfort in the heat and humidity of Panama. "I guess the bangs took the place of the dips of long hair I wore to cover my high forehead," she later told an interviewer. This style never completely changed. The "Mamie Look" of the 1950s included the bangs. Elizabeth Arden, known for her beauty salons and cosmetic products, created a diagram for styling Mamie's hair so that it always looked the same. In a letter to the first lady, Arden assured Mamie that she asked "the young woman who does your hair to study it [the diagram] very carefully . . . and practice, practice, practice! . . . until she has your special hair-do down perfectly." With variations, many American women copied the style, and bangs became popular for girls, too. Of course, not everyone applauded the look. Staff in the picture department at *Life* suggested that "a slightly different hair-do" would frame the first lady's face "to better advantage." To make the point, the staff sent along a picture of a style they thought more becoming. Mamie ignored the advice. She knew that the look suited her, and at least one designer, Arnold Scaasi, agreed. "Her bangs sometimes looked rather strange in photographs, but in person they were very attractive and looked normal and perfectly right. She had a high forehead and she wore her hair in the most flattering way [she could]."[46]

The occasional attempts to remake Mamie Eisenhower's style, to do away with the sentimental charm bracelets or restyle the hair, were blissfully ignored. The first lady knew what suited her, and she would not be swayed. She was not inflexible or "stuffy." She simply knew what she wanted, exhibiting confidence, a sense of humor, and a concerned regard for others in running the White House and dealing with the press. In other words, Mamie Eisenhower was herself. As Mamie began her tenure as first lady, a journalist proclaimed, "Mamie Is Just What Country Ordered."[47]

CHAPTER 4

ENTERTAINING
AT HOME

There is no written job description for what constitutes the position of being first lady, but intrinsic to the institution is the assumption that the woman in the White House will act as hostess. The tone of White House events reflects the individual personalities and tastes of first ladies, and sometimes outside influences such as war or economic downturns may shape public attitudes about what sorts of White House entertainments are appropriate in terms of cost and gaiety. Nevertheless, representing the nation as hostess in the Executive Mansion is an expected duty of the first lady. Mamie Eisenhower considered the role one of her most important. The White House was a symbol of America, and Mamie felt the responsibility of representing the country, whether she was greeting heads of state or the thousands of visitors invited to receptions and other social functions in the Executive Mansion. Mrs. Eisenhower was well prepared for the role, expending much of her time and energy to meet the demands of White House hostess.

In the weeks following Eisenhower's election, attention turned to Mrs. Eisenhower and her plans for the entertaining during the upcoming social season. One national magazine proclaimed that it was going to be a "Gayer White House" that reflected the new first lady's sparkling personality. During the 1930s the Roosevelts hosted formal White House events, and they entertained a number of dignitaries and foreign visitors at Valkill near Hyde Park, New York; it was there that King George and Queen Elizabeth of England, rather cautiously, tried their first hot dogs. During World War II, however, the Roosevelts seldom hosted anything more than small, informal White House dinners with what some Washington insiders joked was the worst food ever served in the Executive Mansion. The Trumans held formal receptions and dinners, but the couple considered these affairs burdensome and something to be endured. Mamie, on the other hand, enjoyed entertaining and intended to bring a luster to White House events. Her first order of business was to "enliven the frosty, stiff official functions" with a style that would make them "more pleasant for all." The White House was now the Eisenhowers' home, and, said Mamie, "I like nothing better than entertaining at home."[1]

Mamie planned to keep a rigorous social schedule and to bring glamour to the White House. The first formal reception of the 1953 social season, traditionally held for the diplomatic corps, proved the point. The *Washington Evening Star* gushed that there had not been such a "brilliant and stately reception" in several years. Mamie wrote a friend that besides "miscellaneous engagements," the White House would host "the full social season of receptions and dinners." That meant at least twelve major functions, besides state dinners. And, unlike the Trumans, whom the White House staff had learned simply preferred to be in the right place at the right time, Mamie was completely engaged. Although one reporter said that it was a new experience for the White House florist, a thirty-year veteran, to be called in by the first lady to discuss floral arrangements, it would have been more accurate to say that not since Lou Hoover had the White House staff seen a first lady so concerned with minute details. Mrs. Eisenhower worked with staff on the menus, selected the linens, and worked over the smallest items such as place cards and gift favors.[2]

Mamie was up to the task of performing the obligation of hostess. From the time of their early military days, the Eisenhowers entertained at home, offering an evening of companionship and good fun that often included Mamie playing the piano. While they were in Paris during the 1920s, their apartment became a second home, "Club Eisenhower," to military friends and other Americans visiting Europe. Informal home entertaining was a mainstay of the Eisenhower household. As Ike's career advanced, the Eisenhowers' social obligations expanded, and Mamie's skills were honed in the military culture. Her first true test in what she called "party management" came in Panama when she took on the job of organizing an elegant farewell dinner for General and Mrs. Fox Conner. It took considerable organizational skills to plan a meal, rent china from a nearby hotel, and then convince her friends at the post to lend their linen and silver to the event. As a military wife, Mamie also was expected to assist at teas or receptions sponsored by the post commander and/or his wife. In that environment, she advanced from a junior officer's wife "in charge of [the reception] dining room" to a senior officer's wife standing in receiving lines. "We shook hands with at least 1,000 people—that's no Joke. . . . I foolishly didn't take off my West Point ring consequently I had a bruise on my little finger," she wrote of a 1940 reception at Fort Lewis.[3]

As Mamie prepared to take on the responsibilities of White House hostess, she felt certain that she was more prepared than some would have been. She had lived at three different overseas postings before World War II. In the Philippines, the Eisenhowers mixed with the highest echelons of government officials and social elite, and after World War II, while Ike was at NATO, the Eisenhowers met, entertained, or were the guests of every royal family and European head of government. Of a dinner and reception held at the Palais de l'Elysée, Mamie wrote her mother: "The President [of France] and I led the March into dinner. . . . I wore the light blue taffeta—looked elegant if I do say it myself." On another occasion, while Mrs. Doud and Mamie's sister Mike visited the Eisenhowers in Europe, they were guests of the royal families of the Netherlands and of Sweden. During the Stockholm visit, Mrs. Doud, Mike, and Mamie delighted their hosts with an impromptu after-dinner serenade of Swedish folk songs. Several of the dignitaries Mamie met during Ike's tenure with NATO would later visit the White House as old acquaintances.[4]

Among those friends and acquaintances invited to the Executive Mansion were Princess Beatrix and Prince Bernhard of the Netherlands; Charles de Gaulle; Lord Hastings Lionel Ismay, who served on Churchill's staff during World War II; Sir Winston Churchill; Her Majesty Mary, British queen mother; Prime Minister Harold Macmillan; Madame Chiang Kai-shek, whom Mamie had met on a

*Mamie (far right) and Ike with the British royal family at Balmoral Castle.
When she became first lady, Mamie already knew western Europe's
heads of state, dignitaries, and royal families.
Dwight D. Eisenhower Presidential Library*

number of previous occasions; Indira Gandhi, who was entertained
by the Eisenhowers while Ike was at Columbia University; and Sir
Bernard Montgomery. Of the Montgomery visit, Mamie wrote a
friend: "We had a dinner for Monty the other evening at the White
House, and we got many of our Army friends together. . . . good to
see them, and of course we caught up on lots of news." Montgomery, abrasive and opinionated, was actually one of Mamie's favorite
guests because "he didn't demand anything." Mamie countered his
tart manner with humor. She later told an interviewer that when the
World War II field marshal looked around the first floor of the
White House and said, "Well, it isn't Buckingham Palace," she laughingly responded, "Well, thank goodness for that." Perhaps one of the
most pleasant experiences was the 1956 visit of Queen Elizabeth II
and Prince Philip. "We renewed friendships that went back to 1942,
when the Queen was a very young Crown Princess," said Ike. "This
was one ceremonial visit that we were sorry to see end." President
and Mrs. Eisenhower again renewed their friendship with the British royals when they were guests aboard the royal yacht for the 1959

Queen Elizabeth II and Prince Philip of Great Britain and the Eisenhowers prior
to a state dinner. The Eisenhower White House hosted more heads of state and
foreign dignitaries than any previous administration.
Dwight D. Eisenhower Presidential Library

American-Canadian ceremonies that hailed the opening of the St. Lawrence Seaway. Ike called it another "pleasant visit."[5]

During Eisenhower's two-term presidency, the White House welcomed thirty-seven foreign heads of state, which was more than had been entertained by any previous president. Added to that number were over thirty more official foreign visitors, as well as people important in shaping world events.[6] That so many, from around the world, visited the White House was a reflection of the Eisenhowers' expanded worldview, shaped by their many experiences abroad. Leaders from Japan, Korea, Vietnam, the Philippines, the Middle East, Africa, Canada, Europe, and Central and South America were White House guests. The president believed that face-to-face meetings enhanced the prospects for peace at a time when so many parts of the world were potential powder kegs, and these meetings enhanced the administration's policy of containing communism during the cold war, developing allies in places that were ignored by previous administrations.

Mamie's approach was to provide a comfortable, yet elegant, setting that conveyed respect for the foreign dignitaries. Before a state dinner, she coordinated with the chief usher, chief butler, and housekeeper. By 1960, the three supervised a combined staff of 133. Meanwhile, Mamie insisted that she and Ike go over the seating arrangements to ensure that dinner partners were as compatible as possible. Tables were arranged to form an E. The new arrangement did away with the U-shaped table that dated back to Theodore Roosevelt's administration. Although some considered the U-arrangement "a sacred aspect of White House state dinners," Mrs. Eisenhower disliked the design. It put her back to many of the guests. With the E-shaped table, the Eisenhowers and guests of honor sat in the middle of the E's vertical column and looked over the three branches of the table. With this arrangement, Mamie could see her guests, and no one sat with his or her back to the guest of honor.[7]

Following each state dinner there was entertainment. Many of the early dinners were followed by dancing, but musical presentations soon became the favored end to an evening. As much as possible, the choices were based on the "reported tastes of our foreign visitors," said Ike, although he privately admitted that one of his least favorite choices was the jazz so loved by one visiting dignitary. During the eight years of White House entertaining, there was an eclectic mix of offerings. Leonard Bernstein and the New York Philharmonic Orchestra, Gregor Piatigorsky, Marian Anderson, folk singers, and the National Capital Harp Ensemble performed. Arthur Rubinstein's appearance in May 1957 was the first and only time the pianist performed at the White House. Also invited to perform were the orchestras of Lawrence Welk, Fred Waring, and Guy Lombardo. Military choral groups were a mainstay, but the Eisenhowers also invited popular Broadway stars to perform the songs that constituted what was later considered to be the golden age of the Broadway musical. The Eisenhowers' personal favorites leaned toward dance bands and show tunes, reflecting the popular tastes of American culture, but the programs were selected to please the guests of honor and to showcase the musical spectrum found in American society. Music critics from major newspapers, invited to the after-dinner performance of world-renowned pianist Leon Fleisher, applauded the Eisenhower White House for recognizing "America's standards of musical excellence."[8]

The variety in musical events was overshadowed by those presented in the Kennedy White House, and in the years following the Kennedy administration, a rather negative view of the Eisenhowers' style of entertaining became accepted as fact. Comparisons between the two painted the Eisenhowers as rather drab and unsophisticated. One Mamie biography described the Eisenhower White House as "homespun middle-America," much more like the "stay-at-home Trumans" than the "elegant" Kennedys. In other descriptions, the Eisenhowers have been portrayed as either too ill or too old to do justice to the demands of entertaining in the Executive Mansion. Certainly, there were periods in which health problems curtailed participation in social functions. The most dramatic events occurred when Ike suffered a heart attack in 1955 and had surgery in 1956 for ileitis. Mamie, too, was hospitalized when she underwent a hysterectomy in 1957. (The procedure was delicately described to the press as an operation "typical of women her age.") During these times, the Nixons stepped in to host foreign dignitaries, and Mamie planned her operation for late summer before the formal social season began in the fall. The White House schedule of events was not drastically reduced until the fall 1960 when the Eisenhowers prepared to leave the Executive Mansion, and the elegance that Mamie expected was never compromised.[9]

Observers on the scene, in fact, portrayed a very different picture from that commonly presented in the post-Eisenhower years. J. B. West, whose tenure at the White House extended through the Kennedy administration, wrote: "Mamie Eisenhower as a hostess was spectacular. In her diamonds and décolleté gowns, she fairly sparkled. She and the General brought more spit and polish, more pomp and circumstance, to their lavish, formal entertaining than any other President and First Lady in my White House experience." Journalist Lonnelle Aikman shared much the same viewpoint: "[The Eisenhowers] brought many things to the President's House: The dignity that befits the Presidency and a warmth and informality which typify America as we like to believe in it." More direct was columnist Josephine Ripley's assessment: "Mamie Eisenhower will go down in history as one of the most gracious hostesses the White House has ever had."[10]

Mamie had a knack for making guests feel welcome while, at the same time, finding a balance between comfortable hospitality and the rigid rules of protocol. An integral component to the reception of dignitaries, and often overlooked in general comments regarding the role of first lady, was protocol. There were stringent guidelines for who stood in a receiving line, in what order, and where guests of honor were seated at dinner. When Mamie Eisenhower came to the White House, she was already well schooled in the intricate subject. Her preparation came from her many experiences within the diplomatic circles of the Philippines and postwar Europe, as well as military life, where protocol decided who stood in a receiving line, forms of introduction, and where someone was seated, not only by rank but by date of commission. She knew that "failure to recognize the proper rank and precedence of a guest . . . [was] equivalent to an insult" to the person's position and the country he or she represented. Before the state dinner for the president of Haiti, for example, Mamie feared that he might not be accorded full protocol rights, and interceded through the White House Social Office that coordinated state visits with the State Department. And, when the president of Guatemala was invited to visit the United States, she thought that the dignitary might feel slighted if expected to stay at the embassy or one of Washington's upscale hotels. "If I were invited to London, I would expect to stay at Buckingham," she wrote in a memo. At the very least, she would expect to stay at one of the royal residences such as Clarence House. The visiting president was put at Blair House as "guest adjunct to the White House."[11]

She was just as demanding when it came to correct dress. On the occasion of the visit of the president of the Federal German Republic, a minor incident erupted. It was June, and the proper dress code for after June 1 was white dinner jacket. Invitations for the state dinner specified as such, and the guest of honor had come prepared. It was unseasonably cool, however, and Ike wanted to wear black. Ike's stubbornness—"he literally blew his top"—brought everything to a halt. The matter of the white dinner jacket versus the black "was discussed with the President, Mrs. Eisenhower, the Secretary of State, . . . and thousands of State employees. People just would not believe the furor," recalled Ike's secretary Ann Whitman. Mamie won the debate. The white dinner jacket remained the required dress.[12]

Dress became a problem, too, when Soviet premier Nikita Khrushchev visited in 1959 with his wife, two daughters, son, and son-in-law. Relations between the United States and the Soviet Union were just beginning to thaw, and Khrushchev agreed to visit the United States prior to a summit in Paris. As courtesy demanded, there would be a state dinner, and the first lady, along with the White House staff, worked for weeks going over the details. On the day of the event, Mamie was informed that the Khrushchev party refused to "dress" for dinner. The men would wear business suits; the women, street-length dresses. Khrushchev exhibited mercurial moods on his American tour. One moment he played the jovial tourist; the next instant, he lectured Eisenhower and the press on what he saw as America's wasteful culture of consumption. Not dressing for dinner was a Khrushchev fly-in-the-ointment move designed to upset plans for the White House dinner, but Mamie refused to be bullied or pressured. A state dinner was a formal occasion and would be treated as such. She insisted that Ike wear white tie. She wore a gown of gold brocade by Scaasi. As it turned out, the Soviet premier appeared in formal attire; his wife wore a "simply cut evening gown of iridescent material."[13]

During his U.S. tour, Khrushchev became a "benign and entertaining guest" when he visited the Gettysburg farm. Ike's intention was to show the Soviet leader the domestic side of American life; Mamie, John and Barbara Eisenhower, and the Eisenhower grandchildren were at the farm to meet Khrushchev. As gifts, he gave the children Christmas ornaments. (Barbara Eisenhower would later say that this seemed strange, coming from the leader of a country that expounded atheism.) In addition, Khrushchev suggested that the children accompany their parents and grandparents on a trip to Moscow after the upcoming Paris summit. "The parents," said Ike, "appeared more hesitant but the children were enthusiastic." The trip never took place. Without the family, Ike went to Paris, where the summit failed after an American U-2 spy plane was shot down over Soviet territory, creating an international incident and an outraged response from the Soviet Union.[14]

Mamie did not accompany Ike on the trip to the Paris summit or on his 1959 and 1960 goodwill tours to countries around the world. She disliked flying, and in the case of the multiple stops required for the goodwill trips, she worried that the many takeoffs and landings would aggravate her inner-ear problem and affect her equilibrium.

However, she did travel with Ike on three foreign trips, reversing her usual role of hostess to one of guest. In July 1955, the leaders of the United States, England, France, and the Soviet Union met for a summit in Geneva, Switzerland. Eisenhower wanted to talk about disarmament, reunification of Germany, cultural exchanges between East and West, and the plight of people living under Soviet occupation in Eastern Europe. Less than an hour before leaving for the summit, he addressed the American people, saying that former presidents Wilson and Roosevelt left the continental United States to either meet over plans for war or sign treaties to end war. He was going to "a conference . . . in order to prevent wars." Mamie watched Ike's televised speech from the White House residence with family and friends. When Ike returned, there was little time to do more than head for the plane. "Mamie," wrote Ike, "although she never completely convinced herself that an airplane flies, was bearing up like a good soldier."[15]

It was rare for a sitting president to travel outside the United States. It was rarer still for a first lady to accompany her husband. Eleanor Roosevelt traveled with FDR to Monterrey, Mexico, when he met with President Avila Camacho in 1943, and she went with her husband to the Second Quebec Conference in 1944. Bess Truman, along with daughter Margaret, traveled with President Truman in 1947 to Brazil. Shortly after Mamie became first lady, she accompanied Ike out of the country in 1953 for a three-day trip to Ottawa, where the president addressed the Canadian Parliament, and she went to Ottawa again in 1958 when Ike met with the Canadian prime minister to discuss trade relations. Her trip to Geneva was, however, the first time that a first lady traveled on a diplomatic trip to Europe while her husband was in office. That Mamie agreed to make the trip, and to go by plane, underlined the importance Ike attached to the meeting. Her presence, he later said, made "a great though unofficial contribution."[16]

On the first leg of the journey, the Eisenhowers, with staff and son John, stopped in Iceland, where the president of the country gave a dinner in their honor. Prior to reaching Geneva, Ike told Mamie and the others that he expected a welcome appropriate to protocol. They were met instead with an "exceptional ceremony of welcome." Mrs. Eisenhower had little contact with the summit participants, and her only meeting with the Soviet delegation came when Ike gave a small dinner party for the group at the villa used by the Eisenhowers while in Geneva. None of the Soviet wives accompanied their husbands to the summit, so Mamie greeted the delegation when it arrived at the villa and "then, according to plan, she withdrew before dinner." While Ike was engaged during several days of summit talks and meetings, Mamie and the wives of the British prime minister and French premier were escorted on sightseeing tours and were guests of honor at luncheons and teas. The press made a great deal out of the first lady's middle name, Geneva, and used numerous flattering adjectives to describe her. "The Swiss press," observed the *New York Times*, "seems to have adopted Mrs. Eisenhower as its special favorite. In headlines she is always 'Mamie.'" Her presence at Geneva was important to Ike, and as first lady, she admirably carried out the role of representing the United States in a "genteel" and "charming" manner. Mamie was rather succinct in her own description of the summit. In a letter to friend Kitty Smith, she did not focus on her activities or contributions, but simply wrote: "Our trip to Switzerland was ever so interesting but terribly busy and hectic. We are grateful to be back home safe and sound."[17]

Formal state dinners and evening receptions were the glittering centerpieces to Mamie's job as a hostess, but other social events received little press coverage. The first lady held teas for the wives of men serving in the House of Representatives, and for the women who were elected representatives. Mamie invited the wives of cabinet members and agency heads to luncheons. Many of her afternoons were spent greeting tour groups and hosting receptions. Writing to her friend Grace Gruenther, Mamie noted: "We have been in a busy whirl. . . . We entertained Their Majesties, King Paul and Queen Fredericka [of Greece] . . . and then followed in quick succession our dinner for the Cabinet and the Diplomatic Reception. And of course inbetween every day I have groups of ladies coming in by the two and three hundred's." During the early months of her first year in the White House, Mamie confided to a friend, "April and May have been my two hardest months. I have asked Mrs. McCaffree today to count up the many hands I have shaken for the last six or eight weeks. After yesterday's 1300, Friday's 3000, Thursday's 1200,

Mamie and the wives of the French president and British prime minister on a
sightseeing tour during the Geneva Summit.
Dwight D. Eisenhower Presidential Library

the right member is a little weak!" To another friend she wrote that
during a five-day period she shook hands with about 6,000 women.
The numbers were not an exaggeration. *Newsweek* reported that
during Mamie's first four years in the White House, she shook hands
with at least 100,000 people.[18]

The records of the White House Social Office confirm that the
first lady welcomed a startling number of special tours representing
a cross section of clubs, professional organizations, and interests.

Not all were women's organizations, but at least half were. Among them were the National Association of Colored Women, the National Association of Deans of Women, the National League of American Pen Women, the American Council of Railroad Women, the Civil Defense National Women's Advisory Council, and women delegates to the United Nations. Mrs. Eisenhower often greeted these groups alone, but she made a concerted effort, from the first days of arriving in the White House, to include Mrs. Nixon. Two days after the 1953 inauguration, for instance, she invited Pat to join her in receiving about 800 women at a reception. Mrs. Nixon was also on hand when the White House hosted one of its largest single receptions, held for the Daughters of the American Revolution. Approximately 4,000 representatives were invited to tea in 1953, and Mamie asked seven wives of government officials to assist, including Pat Nixon, who considered it an honor. The event was well received, despite the "very undignified spectacle" of DAR members "sitting on newspapers on the curb" waiting to get into the White House. Eleven years later, when Lady Bird Johnson invited the same group, she wondered how Mamie had managed the throng, and Mrs. Johnson invited a limited guest list of 200.[19]

Mamie considered the White House to be the People's House. Tourists came through during morning tours. Special tours often followed in the afternoon. The first lady sometimes simply greeted the latter from the staircase, but more often than not, there was a receiving line. As she welcomed the visitors, Mamie found something to say to each person. It might be a compliment on a hat or piece of jewelry, or she might comment on the town or state that the person represented. She had, after all, been to most states during the 1952 campaign. "If there were a thousand people going through the line," recalled J. B. West, "she'd have a thousand little items of small talk for them. In fact, she could charm the socks off anybody she met." Mamie also had an uncanny memory for names and faces. In one instance, she greeted three groups of women scheduled for an afternoon reception. At the end of the receiving line was a woman who had attended an earlier reception and wanted to test the first lady's memory. When Mamie saw her, she said, "What! You here again!" The crowd loved it. What the public did not realize was the toll these receptions sometimes exacted. The Reverend Edward Elson, pastor

Mamie and a group of high school students from South Carolina visiting the
White House. National Park Service Photograph by Abbie Rowe,
Courtesy Dwight D. Eisenhower Presidential Library

of the National Presbyterian Church attended by the Eisenhowers,
visited Mamie a day after a White House function. "Her entire fore-
arm and hand, as well as her ankles and feet, were swollen, the result of shaking hands with hundreds of people at a White House
ceremony. . . . But she had uncomplainingly carried on." During the
second term, Ike tried to dissuade Mamie from shaking hands at receptions. "[She] insists on talking to everyone," he said. "It's a strain
on her."[20]

The White House had a no-smoking rule in place for large receptions. This had nothing to do with being concerned with second-
hand smoke or the social correctness of not lighting up. The U.S.
surgeon general was years away from making any statement on
smoking being bad for one's health, although a 1952 research report
suggested a link between cigarettes and cancer. The ban on smoking
was based on the fire marshal's concern that so many people at a reception, many of them smoking, were a fire hazard. During the Truman administration, ushers began to politely ask guests to put out

their cigarettes, citing the fire marshal's fears. The policy continued in the Eisenhower White House, although Mamie gave another reason for the rule. Many of the guests' dresses were of man-made fabrics, rayon or nylon, and there was all that net and chiffon that could easily burn. It was a disaster waiting to happen. "You could start a terrible fire that way," she explained.[21]

Mamie herself smoked in private, and she was not the only first lady to smoke. Eleanor Roosevelt lit up after dinner, signaling guests that they could do the same, and at formal dinners Jacqueline Kennedy had cigarettes available at each place setting. Grace Coolidge, Jacqueline Kennedy, Pat Nixon, Betty Ford, and Nancy Reagan smoked, but they were seldom, if ever, seen in public with a cigarette. If the opposite had been true, there probably would have been little public outcry. Women had been smoking openly for most of the twentieth century. Suffrage activists did it. Flappers made it a signature act of being a modern woman, and film stars smoked on screen. By the 1950s, women made up the majority of smokers in America. Movie stars appeared in advertisements for cigarette companies, and television personalities such as Lucille Ball and her side-kick, Vivian Vance, lit up on camera. As for Mamie, she continued to smoke even when Ike quit in 1949, and it was several years after she left the White House before she gave it up.[22]

To Mamie, White House guests were "all friends." She did not want to know their religious and political beliefs. Nor did she want entertaining to be "a political issue." She was determined to be a nonpolitical hostess. If others wanted to make that sort of statement, it was their prerogative, but it was not the way she went about entertaining. "I liked that person for what they were—my guest," she explained. To Mamie's way of thinking, a good hostess thought of her guests' comfort and enjoyment, not their political ideologies. Visitors responded in kind. "I think it is so wonderful the way you make everyone feel so much at home," wrote Jacqueline Kennedy. Still, it was impossible for Mamie to remain unaware of where guests' loyalties lay. Jacqueline Kennedy was a newcomer to the White House ritual of senate wives' luncheons, but her husband was pointedly recognized by Ike in 1954 when the president took time during a speech to the National Council of Catholic Women to wish the senator a speedy recovery from surgery. (Both Rose and Jacqueline Kennedy conveyed their thanks for the president's thoughtfulness with effusive letters.) Lady Bird Johnson's political allegiance was even more difficult to overlook. Besides receptions and senate wives' luncheons, Mrs. Johnson attended state dinners when her husband served as senate majority leader. The Johnsons appeared on the guest lists of seven such events, including those for the king and queen of Nepal, President Charles de Gaulle of France, and Queen Elizabeth II. This does not suggest, of course, that Mrs. Eisenhower was on intimate terms with these women. When Mrs. Johnson was first lady, she recorded in her diary that while her husband visited Eisenhower in the hospital in 1968, she had an hour's visit with Mamie, "the longest I've ever had." Lady Bird called it a "pleasant, delightful hour," concluding "what a lucky man [Eisenhower] is to have her constantly at his side."[23]

The senate wives' lunch was a tradition by the time Mamie Eisenhower came to the White House. In 1917, when the United States entered World War I, "senate ladies" began to meet each week to roll bandages and sew for the Red Cross. Wives of current senators, widows of former senators, and women elected to the Senate were included in the group loosely referred to as "senate ladies" or "senate wives." The wife of the vice president presided over the group. In the 1920s Grace Coolidge invited "Ladies of the Senate" to lunch, and Eleanor Roosevelt began hosting a picnic lunch for the group in the 1930s. The luncheons were customary by the time Mamie became first lady. Those attending the luncheons at the Eisenhower White House came away with high compliments for Mamie. In one of her weekly newspaper columns, Dorothy Bush, wife of Senator Prescott Bush and mother of George H. W. Bush, noted Mamie's generous hospitality, and Charity Martin, wife of Senator Edward Martin, wrote, "As always you [Mamie] . . . made everyone feel at ease." There is no record that former first ladies Eleanor Roosevelt or Bess Truman ever attended these events, but Edith Wilson attended on at least one occasion, sharing the receiving line with Mrs. Eisenhower.[24]

Another White House tradition was the garden party for disabled veterans. Edith Wilson held the first in 1919, hosting 800 convalescing World War I soldiers and sailors from nearby military hospitals. The custom was discontinued during World War II and then revived

President and Mrs. Eisenhower greet guests at the 1953 White House garden party
for disabled veterans. United Press Photo

by Bess Truman after the White House renovation was completed.
Along with the veterans and a number of military and government
officials, it was customary to invite Mrs. Wilson. She appeared for
the first Eisenhower garden party, but her staunch loyalty to the
Democratic Party led her to decline several invitations to the Republican White House. Mamie, however, never stopped inviting Mrs.
Wilson to social functions, coaxing her in one instance to attend the
veterans' party because the event "would never be quite complete
without you, its founder." Although Edith considered Mamie "the

most thoughtful friend in the world," she felt that too many appearances at the Republican White House implied support for its policies. Mamie accepted Mrs. Wilson's position and continued to consider her a good friend.[25]

Perhaps taking a cue from Mrs. Wilson's idea for a garden party, Mamie added another in 1959 when she invited residents of several Washington, D.C., area institutions. This included the Washington Home for the Blind, the U.S. Soldiers' Home, and more than twenty denominational and fraternal institutions that cared for senior citizens. Another first was a reunion of first families. Attending were the grandchildren of Harrison and Hoover, and the children of Grant, both Roosevelts, Taft, Wilson, and Coolidge. When Mrs. Johnson repeated the event in 1966, Mamie attended, along with daughter-in-law, Barbara, and granddaughters, Anne, Susan, and Mary Jean.[26]

Reared in a household that loved to commemorate holidays and birthdays, Mamie no longer carried on the Doud family tradition of marching to "Here Comes the Bride" on her birthday, but her love of celebrations continued. She had the housekeeper keep a birthday calendar of the staff, and the White House kitchen made a cake for each person on his or her birthday. The boxed cake, with a personal note from the first lady, could be taken home and shared with the staff member's family. The Eisenhowers' grandchildren also enjoyed birthdays at the White House. In addition to family affairs held in the private residence, Ike and Mamie gave each grandchild one birthday party in the ground-floor library. The guest of honor made up the guest list of school friends. The only formality, said Ike, "was the 'receiving line,' established at the moment when my wife and I appeared at the party. Each youngster was gravely presented to us by the guest of honor." Then, there was cake, ice cream, and entertainment. Each child's party was distinctive. For David, who had the first party, Roy Rogers and Dale Evans, at that time stars of their own television show, sang a few songs. "I am sure that they have never had a noisier or more enthusiastic audience," said Ike.[27]

Another sort of family party occurred near the end of the Eisenhowers' stay in the White House. Ellen and Mamie Moore, the daughters of Mamie's sister Mike, made their debut into society at a

White House tea in 1960. The word *tea* does not adequately describe the event. This was not a tea where a few women sat around sipping from china cups and munching on cucumber sandwiches. This was a lavish affair with tables of food, champagne punch, and 500 guests who included the wives and daughters of foreign ambassadors. The White House affair was covered by *Life* magazine, which quoted Mamie as saying, "If I had two daughters, this is the way I would like them to come out." The event put the first lady in mind of the sort of debut she recalled from her younger days "when you were introduced to your parents' old friends." A Washington newspaper called the event "a historic one for the White House." Not only was it hosted by the wife of the president, but former first lady Edith Wilson was in attendance, along with Alice Roosevelt Longworth, daughter of President Theodore Roosevelt. Well known for her antics as the president's daughter and later as a popular Washington hostess, Mrs. Longworth regaled guests and reporters with stories of her own 1902 society debut at a dance in the White House.[28]

Mamie loved parties that included family, and she displayed the same enthusiasm for holidays. Earlier first ladies had decorated the Executive Mansion at Christmas, but Mamie set the precedent for lavishly decorating the first floor, and she was the first to initiate a Christmas party for *all* White House employees, their spouses, and the Eisenhowers' personal staff. The daytime party served coffee, doughnuts, and coffee cake to an average of 500 guests each year during the Eisenhowers' tenure in the White House. As gifts, employees received one of the commemorative Christmas gift folders produced by Hallmark Cards. Each contained a reproduction of one of President Eisenhower's paintings. There was also a Christmas party for senior staff and members of the cabinet. E. Frederic Morrow, administrative officer for special projects and one of the few top-ranking African Americans in the Eisenhower administration, recalled that for one party Philip Young, chairman of the Civil Service Commission, decided that he and seven members of the president's staff, including Morrow, would play Christmas carols using Young's collection of English bells. With only two days to practice, the results were hilarious. "The President and Mrs. Eisenhower broke up completely," said Morrow. During Ike's second term, there was also a Christmas party for the children of staff; this

The Eisenhowers at one of their White House parties for senior West Wing staff and their spouses. Dwight D. Eisenhower Presidential Library

included the children of the White House police, Secret Service, groundskeepers, garage mechanics, and maintenance workers. As Mamie's granddaughter Mary Jean once observed, Mamie taught inclusion by example. She and Ike took pride in the fact that they knew everyone by name, and in a sense, Mamie considered the staff an extension of family. "They were our friends," she said.[29]

When social functions fell near the time of a holiday, appropriate decorations flourished. At one senate wives' luncheon, for instance, Easter bunnies and eggs took center stage while the idea of spring was conveyed with cherry blossoms and the taped sounds of chirping birds. (The birds were so loud that Mrs. Eisenhower finally asked the usher to turn down the volume.) The Easter holiday also saw revival of the White House Easter Egg Roll in 1953. Discontinued by the Roosevelts during World War II, the traditional event was not reintroduced by the Trumans after the White House renovation. The *New York Times* offered the opinion that President Truman had not reinstated the event because he thought the whole thing "a waste of food." When Mamie announced that the roll would be held, she

*Mamie's love for holiday celebrations included parties for staff, friends, and
family. In this Christmas photograph, Ike and Mamie are shown with son, John,
daughter-in-law Barbara, and grandchildren Anne, Mary Jean, David, and
Susan. National Park Service Photograph by Abbie Rowe,
Courtesy Dwight D. Eisenhower Presidential Library*

called it a "worthwhile tradition." Her son John had taken part years
before, when he was four years old, and now his children would have
the opportunity to participate. "David and Anne joined in the fun,"
Mamie wrote friend Perle Mesta, but it was decided that Susan was
too young. She "watched through the window."[30]

The Easter Egg Roll was open to children aged twelve and younger. Mamie did not make an issue of the fact that the event was integrated, and the press did not comment, making it difficult to ascertain if this was the first time that it was. In the context of the period, however, it is important to note that during the first months of Ike's presidency, the administration immediately began to address integration at schools attended by military dependents (including those serving military posts in the South), and it dealt with integrating schools, restaurants, hotels, theaters, and store lunch counters in Washington, D.C. Although Mamie appeared to have little, if any, interest in such matters, her actions proved otherwise. Besides holding an integrated Easter Egg Roll, she included newswoman Alice A. Dunnigan in media and White House events; she was an honorary member of the National Council of Negro Women; and she invited Mahalia Jackson to perform at one of her birthday celebrations. She supported Ike's decision to send federal troops to enforce integration at Central High in Little Rock, Arkansas, and she sent a heartfelt letter of condolence to the National Association of Colored Women upon the death of the organization's first president, Mary Church Terrell. There was also a special effort to accommodate African American groups, such as the 4-H Club Camp for Negro Boys and Girls, for special White House tours. In her own way, Mamie adopted her husband's "hidden hand" approach. Ike's method, wrote political scientist Fred I. Greenstein, was to operate behind the scenes. He "went to great lengths to conceal the political side of his leadership." Ike did this so well, noted Greenstein, that until the late twentieth century, "most writers on the presidency viewed him through the lens of his 1950s liberal critics."[31]

The same could be said of the public's perception of Mamie, who made no effort to be seen as a socially conscious activist. Another case in point, and one for which Ike's "hidden hand" approach is often cited, was Senator Joseph McCarthy and his hunt for communists. Mamie always maintained that political ideology and partisanship were left at the door when she entertained, but a clear message was sent when she invited Lucille Ball and Desi Arnaz to the White House shortly after Ball was called before the House Committee on Un-American Activities. Accused of being a communist, on the basis of a 1936 voter registration card, Ball testified and was later cleared.

Jack Gould of the *New York Times* wrote that Ball had been very "lucky" when the committee quickly cleared her name; the same could not be said for the experiences of so many others. There was no guarantee, however, that Ball and Arnaz would be able to save their reputations and continue their popular television show. Other careers had been wrecked by just the whiff of innuendo. Then, the invitation came. It was Ike's birthday. Would they entertain? Arnaz later wrote that the president and Mrs. Eisenhower, along with "their VIP guests," gave the couple "a wonderful welcome." At the dinner that followed, Lucy and Desi were seated with the Eisenhowers. After what the couple had gone through, with the future of their careers still somewhat shaky, to be invited to the White House and so warmly received left Arnaz with one thought, "God bless America!" Mamie could have brushed aside any questions on the choice of guests with the truthful statement that *I Love Lucy* was a favorite television show in the Eisenhower household, but the timing also signaled support for the couple in the face of McCarthy's witch hunt.[32]

The Eisenhowers included family and friends in birthday and anniversary parties, and the couple, in keeping with their military past and sense of loyalty to Ike's army friends, invited Ike's West Point classmates (the class of 1915) and their spouses to a formal White House dinner during each of the president's two terms. The dinners were held in conjunction with one of the couple's wedding anniversaries. After the 1954 dinner and evening of music provided by two military bands, Mamie invited the women to see the private residence. "You were darling to invite the ladies up to the second floor," wrote one guest. "We so appreciated your kind thoughtfulness and were very interested to see those lovely rooms." With the exception of the inhabitants of the West Wing, Mamie was not adverse to sharing the family's quarters, and weekends often found the Eisenhowers' "gang" of close friends there. Ike and his bridge group staked out the Monroe Room. Mamie and her friends claimed the solarium for Bolivia, a form of canasta. "We gals have been having some Bolivia, in fact we are going to play tonight!" Mamie wrote one of her absent card-playing friends. Often these informal get-togethers included the president cooking hamburgers or steaks on a grill on the White House roof or making stew in the third-floor kitchen.[33]

Mamie had scores of friends who visited with her in the White House, including the wives of government and cabinet officials, but many of her closest friends were the ones she had known for years. "They are the ones," reported one newspaper in 1957, "who quietly come and go unannounced at the White House." Among these confidantes were Ruth Butcher; Kate Hughes, whose husband, Everett, had been with Ike at the War Department and then with him during World War II; Ann Nevins, who met Mamie in 1936 when they were aboard the same military transport headed for the Philippines; Grace Gruenther, whose husband followed Ike at NATO; Caroline Walker, widow of General Walton Walker; the Baroness Rosemary Silvercruys, a friend from Mrs. Truman's Spanish class; Alice Snyder, wife of Ike's personal physician; and Mary Allen, who had known Mamie since their days in wartime Washington and, with her husband, George, was a Gettysburg neighbor. Also visiting Mamie in the White House were Lydia Taylor, wife of General Maxwell Taylor, and Emily Ord, whose husband was one of Ike's closest friends before his death in the Philippines. There were others who visited with Mamie on a regular basis, but as the women listed here suggest, many of Mamie's most trusted friends shared her background as a military wife. Similar life experiences formed a common bond.[34]

The "gang" that visited the Eisenhowers in the family residence at the White House was also welcome at Gettysburg. After her first visit to the farm, friend Priscilla Slater wrote: "It was fun to see their joy in having a place of their own at last and their anticipation to live in it was evident." As in the White House, there was a great deal of card playing at Gettysburg, and dinners often included Ike's cooking. "We had dinner outside . . . and the President's steaks were cooked in the charcoal," wrote Dr. Howard Snyder in his daily accounts of Ike's activities. On another occasion he noted that the Eisenhowers and their guests played cards for two hours in the afternoon and then "after dinner, bridge and Bolivia was resumed. They played until midnight." Friends and family mingled at these casual gatherings, and the farm was also a place for quiet family celebrations. "Friday will be Mother's birthday," Mamie wrote a friend in 1955, "and she wishes to spend the day up at Gettysburg. All the Moores [sister Mike's family] will come up for the day for a real family celebration!"[35]

The Pennsylvania farm was for friends and family. On rare occasions dignitaries such as Khrushchev and Winston Churchill visited there, and in 1956 Ike launched his reelection bid at the farm, hosting 500 top-level Republicans at a tent-covered picnic. Although Mamie tried to keep the same distance between home and work that she enforced in the White House, she was proud of her new home and wanted to show it off. A picnic for Oveta Culp Hobby when she left her cabinet post provided the opportunity for members of Ike's cabinet to see the farm, and two picnics, one in each of the president's terms in office, included every employee of the White House. No matter the job—carpenter, electrician, telephone operator, kitchen worker—and no matter the racial or ethnic background of individuals, everyone was invited. A few employees, including some of the electricians and carpenters and usher J. B. West, saw the house as it was being constructed. Undoubtedly, others heard a great deal about it as Mamie fussed over measurements for curtains and the trials of having furniture upholstered. In the case of the employee picnics, the Eisenhowers wanted to share their new home with those they relied upon in the Executive Mansion.[36]

The private side of White House life centered on friends and family. Mamie's mother continued to maintain her home in Denver after the death of John Doud in 1951, but she periodically lived at the White House until her death in 1960. Mamie wanted her mother at the Executive Mansion, fretting whenever Elivera returned to Denver. On more than one occasion, Mamie "prevailed upon her to stay a little longer." The two acted more like girlfriends than mother and daughter, said Kate Hughes. Both women shared a sense of humor and fun, as Eisenhower friend Ellis Slater recorded when he presented them with fancy umbrellas on an Easter Sunday. "They were pleased," he wrote, "and paraded in the living room as if they were Parisian models."[37]

When Elivera was in residence, Mamie's morning work from bed was often interrupted by a telephone call from her mother—who was in her own room reading or watching television. "Excuse me," Mamie would say to head usher West or Mary Jane McCaffree, "I have a long-distance call from mother." Ike enjoyed having Elivera in residence. His relationship with both Douds was always a "mutual admiration society," and he considered his mother-in-law a "close friend." He teasingly called her "Min" after a character in the "Andy Gump" comic strip, and when there was no social engagement scheduled for the evening, the three often ate dinner in front of the television in the family residence.[38]

Then, there were the visits from the grandchildren. These, said Ike, were "highlights to our domestic life." Despite the demands of office, Ike and Mamie made time to enjoy the role of grandparent, and they loved doing things with, and for, the children. On one occasion in 1954, they promised to take the children for a boat ride on the Potomac, but as the scheduled time for departure neared, it began to rain. Ike "grabbed up the phone and called Bill Draper to get an Air Force report on the weather," recalled press secretary James Hagerty. Learning that the weather would clear within the hour, Ike "wiped some imaginary sweat off his forehead" and said, "David and the girls would never have understood it if we hadn't gone this afternoon." The children sometimes stayed at the White House, either alone or with their parents. While John and Barbara Eisenhower prepared for their 1954 move to Fort Leavenworth, where John was to attend the Command and General Staff College, the children stayed at the White House. "You know how much fun we are going to have!" Mamie wrote a friend. And, at another time, Mamie was looking forward to the children's stay so that "I can cuddle [five-month-old] Mary Jean to my heart's content." The youngest of the grandchildren, Mary Jean had the distinction of being one of the few children ever christened in the White House. Whether visiting over a weekend or staying for a few days, the children brought youthful vitality to the Executive Mansion. For the first time since FDR, said *Life* magazine, the White House "echoed to the scampering of presidential grandchildren."[39]

The children played in the third-floor toy room, watched movies in the theater, and swam in the pool. When one of their parakeets died, it was given a burial (and tombstone) near the Rose Garden. "Roads through the South Grounds," recalled Ike, "became proving grounds for bicycles and the electric carts [a miniature Thunderbird car] given to the children by friends." And, "the ground floor of the Mansion itself was far from immune to use by the grandchildren as a race track." They were allowed on the ground floor after morning tours ended, but Mamie's rules "were to be strictly obeyed," recalled granddaughter Susan. "No running up and down corridors, no sliding down banisters, no greasy fingers on the woodwork, no getting down from the table before the meal was over." Mamie had her rules, but both she and Ike were indulgent grandparents. Grandson David fondly recalled playing hide-and-seek in her bedroom, and granddaughter Anne described her as "extremely playful."[40]

The Mamie that her family and friends knew was much the same as the one who greeted foreign dignitaries or welcomed the thousands who walked through the White House doors for tours or receptions. A stickler for protocol and a perfectionist regarding details, she nevertheless managed to put guests at ease and add sparkle to the White House. A friend and sometime guest at formal White House functions described Mamie as possessing "an unusual combination of warmth and enthusiasm" that was "almost girlish." At the same time, she maintained "the dignity befitting the President's wife." Virginia Conner, who had been a White House guest during at least three previous administrations, told Mamie that upon her first visit during the Eisenhowers' tenure, "the minute I entered [the White House] I felt a complete change in the atmosphere. . . . the way things are run is remarkable." Mrs. Eisenhower brought humor, style, and a sense of elegance to the first lady's role of hostess. It was a responsibility that she considered most important among the many expected of her. "I personally think," said Ike, "that Mamie's biggest contribution [as first lady] was to make the White House livable, comfortable, and meaningful for the people who came in. . . . She exuded hospitality. She saw that as one of her functions and performed it, no matter how tired she was. In the White House you need intelligence and charm—to make others glad to be around you. She had that ability."[41]

CHAPTER 5

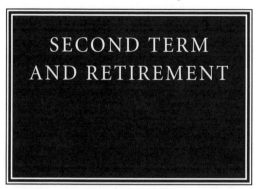

SECOND TERM AND RETIREMENT

During the early hours of September 24, 1955, President Eisenhower suffered a heart attack while vacationing with Mamie at the Doud home in Denver. Ike thought the severe chest pains were indigestion. Mamie thought they were something more serious and called Dr. Howard Snyder, the president's personal physician. The doctor administered several kinds of medications, but he did not contact a cardiologist at Fitzsimons Army Hospital until the morning of the twenty-fourth. Hours later, Ike was taken to the hospital. Mamie moved into a nearby room and during the first days relied heavily upon her son, who immediately flew to be at his parents' side. Mamie also reached out to close friends. Writing to Louise Caffey, she could only say: "It was all so sudden and came as such a shock."[1]

Behind the scenes other doctors questioned Dr. Snyder's handling of the situation, but the controversy became secondary to notifying the press and the American people. Initially, the press was told that the problem was indigestion, but this was rather quickly revised to "mild" heart attack. On Monday, September 26, the news sent the stock market plummeting. When Ike recovered enough in the hospital to speak with his son and staff, he insisted that the public be told the whole truth. He recalled that President Woodrow Wilson's long illness was misrepresented to the public, leading some to wonder if Edith Wilson and a small "White House palace guard"

were running the country. He wanted Americans to be reassured
that the government was functioning, with Vice President Nixon
holding scheduled cabinet meetings and administration staff con-
ducting business as usual. Dr. Paul Dudley White, a renowned cardiologist, was called in to consult. Later, his press conference gave "the
nation a course on myocardial infarction." Updates told the public
what was being done, and this seemed to offer reassurance that
modern medicine would restore the president's health. The reports
were candid up to a point, and Ike's insistence that the whole truth
be told had its limitations. The public was not told that the heart attack was massive or that there was a cardiac aneurysm. It was little
wonder that Mamie later said, "After 1955, whenever Ike gave a speech,
I always sat there in utter dread that he would have a heart attack on
the air."[2]

On November 11, Ike was allowed to return to Washington, where
he stayed two days before going with Mamie to Gettysburg to conva-
lesce. "I would be available to official visitors," he explained, "but not
too easily available to people who just 'wanted to see the President.'"
A month later, the Eisenhowers returned to the White House. In the
interim, Pat and Richard Nixon took on the responsibilities of official hosts to the president of Guatemala, the president of Uruguay,
and the president of Italy. The Nixons had substituted for the Eisenhowers on earlier occasions, and Pat and Mamie had formed a relationship that went beyond the formalities of their roles. While Ike
was still hospitalized, Pat wrote to Mamie: "I did want you to know
that our thoughts and prayers have been with you constantly. . . . I
just wish there was some way I could lighten your burdens. At any
rate, please know that you have my admiration and love."[3]

Ike's health added a question mark to the speculation that he
would run for a second term. Just seven months earlier, however, it
was Mamie's health that created a small sensation. The *New York
Times* told the story with headlines that read "2 Parties in Clash on
Mrs. Eisenhower." Paul M. Butler, Democratic national chairman
and staunch Adlai Stevenson supporter, precipitated the story by
saying that he understood Ike would not run again "because of a
personal situation in the Eisenhower household." Butler hinted that
Mamie was drinking. After outraged Republicans repudiated the
story, Butler tempered his earlier remarks by saying that he had

heard through a White House "leak" that Mrs. Eisenhower was un-well. In fact, Mamie had been in bed for several days with the flu, but when Dr. Snyder decided to elaborate on the first lady's health by tell-ing reporters that she had "a slight heart condition," he only made matters worse. Press secretary Hagerty asked the doctor to please leave talking to reporters to him. Within a few days the flurry sub-sided, and Butler came off badly in the press. By March 13, the *New York Times* reported that Mamie was well enough to attend a small dinner party for Robert Cutler, who was leaving his job as special as-sistant to the president on national security and returning to his banking business in Boston. Nevertheless, Ike was still furious, telling Hagerty that Butler's behavior was "about as low as it can come." Then, thinking of his own political plans, he added, "I suppose that Mrs. Ike would like to get up to that farm, but I am sure that she will not make the final decision but will leave that entirely to me."[4]

When she was a young wife of an army officer, Mamie learned that Ike considered his first duty was to the military and to his coun-try. Mamie could wield influence over Ike, but she would never chal-lenge his sense of serving something larger than himself. Just as Mamie saw herself as a partner in Ike's military career, she accepted the principle that she and Ike were serving their country. Mamie be-lieved that the choice to seek a second term was Ike's, but she did not simply sit on the sidelines, waiting for him to decide. Eisenhower's brother Milton, son John, and close friend George Allen took the position that Ike could "increase his prospects for longevity" by not seeking a second term. Mamie, on the other hand, said Ike, "thought idleness would be fatal for one of my temperament; consequently, she argued that I should listen to my most trusted advisers, and then make my own decision." Mamie had just been dealing with Ike's pe-riodic fits of depression during his convalescence at Gettysburg. A common aftereffect in cardiac patients, Ike's occasional complaints of feeling suddenly old and ineffectual most likely had some effect on Mamie's reasoning. Ultimately, Ike had to choose. Mamie said that she would support him whatever the decision. John later wrote that he was surprised that his mother would agree to another cam-paign, but she had "an almost mystical feeling" that Ike had more to do. "I just can't believe that Ike's work is finished," she said. Mamie's attitude bolstered her husband. In his memoirs, he later wrote:

"Mamie above all others, never accepted the assumption that I had incurred a disabling illness. . . . she perhaps more than any other retained the conviction that my job as president was not finished."[5]

Mamie's feelings were based on faith in her husband and personal religious convictions. Neither she nor Ike thought it proper to parade their religious faith for public view, but she expressed herself in many ways other than the couple's attendance at National Presbyterian Church in Washington. In small, quiet acts, she made declarations of faith. She put a plaque with a prayer and a picture of the Virgin Mary on the wall of the White House kitchen; the staff "was flattered rather than perturbed." In addition, she asked the Reverend Edward Elson to bless the house at Gettysburg with a brief service; a plaque was placed at the door to commemorate the blessing. Mamie's personal beliefs were private, but during the postpresidential years her comments to interviewers provided some insight to her thoughts. She told Barbara Walters that her philosophy was that "God's not going to let anything happen to him [Ike] until he's finished the work that He's sent him to do." She felt that way during the war years, and she continued to believe it through Ike's health crises during the presidency.[6]

Her deeply felt convictions nevertheless battled with her tendency to worry and to fear the worst. The death of their child Ikky, as well as the early demise of her two sisters, left Mamie with a heightened sense of disaster looming just around the corner. She told biographer Dorothy Brandon that her "close guardianship" of her son while he was growing up "amounted almost to a phobia." She was terrified that he would be injured playing sports or "contract some serious illness." When he was sent to Korea, she "no longer worried about his health—he had that in abundance. It was his very life that was at stake, if a 'numbered' bullet or piece of shrapnel found its mark." That was a very real concern for all who had loved ones in Korea, but Mamie's fears were accentuated by a lifetime of what she acknowledged bordered on smothering watchfulness. After the grandchildren came along, her concerns extended to them. She worried that wet hair after pool swims would lead to colds, and when they were driven somewhere by the Secret Service, Mamie always cautioned, "Drive very carefully. Let's have no more tragedies." The loss of her own young child, as well as the deaths of her sisters, never left her.[7]

Given Mamie's personal fears, her acceptance of Ike's decision to seek a second term was all the more remarkable. She held to the belief that Ike had more to contribute, keeping her concerns largely to herself. Letters to friends shortly after Ike announced on February 29, 1956, that he would run, were light and breezy. To an old friend from military days, she wrote: "Well! I've just listened to my husband announce that he will be a candidate for the Republicans again! Naturally, anything he decided to do would be all right with me." Mamie's support, said one reporter, was another example of her being a "good soldier" for her husband's sake.[8]

Five months after Eisenhower made his announcement, another health crisis occurred. He suffered an attack of ileitis, a serious inflammation of the small intestine. When Ike was first hospitalized, doctors differed on whether surgery was necessary. Mamie, fearful of making the wrong decision, could not bring herself to sign the necessary permission papers, even when all finally agreed that an operation was essential. John Eisenhower signed for her. As Ike recovered at Walter Reed Army Hospital, Mamie moved into a small bedroom next to his for the duration of his stay. She ate meals with him, met with the doctors, carefully watched his schedule, and monitored the time visitors had with the president. At the same time, she kept a close check on the White House housekeeping staff, spoke with the head usher every day, went over the mail sent out by her secretary, and answered as many letters as possible. "You would rejoice with me to see the grand progress Ike is making now," she wrote their friends the Gruenthers. Ike's steady progress led to his decision to stay in the race.[9]

The Democrats, once again running Adlai Stevenson as their presidential candidate, planned to make Ike's health an issue of the campaign by questioning his fitness to serve and by targeting Richard Nixon as a person the American people should not accept as being a heartbeat away from the presidency. Nevertheless, a Gallup poll indicated that only 28 percent of voters believed that the president's health should be an issue, and only 30 percent thought there was any likelihood that he would have a heart attack during a second term. Through television and the print media, the image of restored health was reinforced as a smiling, involved presidential candidate appeared at the Republican National Convention in San

Francisco. The *San Francisco Examiner* reported: "A bronzed and jaunty President Eisenhower, with Mamie at his side, came to San Francisco last night and was given a conquering hero's welcome." Five thousand greeted the president's arrival at the airport. Another 12,000 were reported in Union Square chanting for the Eisenhowers to make an appearance at their hotel. "Almost two hours after his arrival [at the St. Francis Hotel]," continued the news report, "the President and Mamie, both grinning like a couple of happy school children, opened a window to the Presidential suite on the sixth floor . . . and waved to the crowd."[10]

The televised convention gave viewers around the country an opportunity to measure the president's healthy appearance, and while strategists decided how television would be used in the campaign, Ike had his own ideas for its convention content. He thought that the hours of airtime should not be filled entirely with speeches. When George Murphy was put in charge of planning entertainment for the event, Ike told the well-known actor and California Republican chairman "to keep the convention moving. . . . there should be enough pure entertainment to give the delegates and the TV audience an occasional change of pace from the political talk." Murphy agreed. Among the entertainers were Ethel Merman, Irene Dunne, and opera diva Patrice Munsel, who sang the national anthem. LeRoy Prinz, onstage coordinator for the convention and one of the directors fired from Cecil B. DeMille's film epic *The Ten Commandments,* quipped: "This [the convention] is my eleventh commandment."[11]

By the end of September, and one year after his heart attack, Ike was on the campaign trail. After making a televised speech, he went to Iowa and then Illinois, where he made a major speech on farm issues. After a brief return to Washington, he made a one-day swing through Ohio and Kentucky. Of later trips, Ann Whitman wrote that there were "tremendous" crowds in Minneapolis–St. Paul, Seattle, Portland, and Los Angeles, which "outdid itself as only that city can in screwballs and glamour and enthusiasm." Mamie was with Ike for most of his campaign appearances.[12]

Although the couple actually added more stops than originally planned, the Republican Party leadership agreed that Ike would not have to engage in the marathon of speeches and cross-country travel that marked the 1952 campaign. To augment the president's personal appearances, strategists turned to television. It had been used in the earlier campaign, but its importance was emphasized in Ike's second run. By the 1956 election, more households owned a television. Ad agencies predicted that seven out of every ten voters would have one. With that in mind, the Republicans put more money into paid airtime. To counter any suggestion that television was "a crutch to get an infirm president past a grueling political campaign," Republican strategists declared television the new medium of modern, political campaigns. It was already apparent that television, with its broadcasts of congressional investigative hearings and interview shows like *Meet the Press,* had a major influence on politics. It represented the future for presenting candidates to the American public, bringing the candidates into people's living rooms.[13]

Certainly, Americans were engaged by the wonder of television, and the Eisenhowers were no different. The Trumans were the first to have a television in the White House: the Eisenhowers had two. Among the Eisenhowers' favorite shows were *I Love Lucy, You Bet Your Life,* and *Arthur Godfrey's Talent Scouts.* Ike enjoyed TV westerns, and Mamie was devoted to *As the World Turns.* When the show played, said J. B. West, "I learned to avoid the second floor . . . if I possibly could, for if I went up there I'd be trapped with 'As the World Turns.' You just can't say, 'I'm sorry, I have more important things to do,' to a First Lady—especially Mrs. Eisenhower."[14]

Mamie enjoyed television, and she was the first first lady to be featured in television campaigning. In October 1956 she appeared with Ike for a nationally aired show on which seven women asked the president preplanned questions. Viewers saw Mamie chatting "easily with women from everyday pursuits." The campaign also created the "Mamie" spot. Shown repeatedly in the fall of 1956, this advertisement featured a woman at home looking after her family. From this scene, the image shifted to the White House and first lady while a woman's voice intoned, "Women will decide the election, and they like Ike . . . and here's something else they like—Ike's beloved Mamie." The campaign used Mamie's popularity to its advantage, and the Eisenhowers' domestic devotion was a counterpoint to the divorced Stevenson.[15]

The first lady appeared in another venue when CBS announced that it would air a birthday party for Mrs. Eisenhower on March 22,

1956. (Her fifty-ninth birthday the previous November had gone largely unmarked because she was with Ike while he recuperated at Gettysburg.) Democratic national chairman Paul Butler cried foul and demanded equal air time, arguing that the birthday party, attended largely by wives of government officials, was a thinly disguised political event. That he was rebuffed should have come as no surprise. William S. Paley, head of CBS, not only had been in the psychological warfare division of Eisenhower's Supreme Headquarters during World War II but also was a personal friend. The Democrats would not get equal airtime for what CBS called "nonpolitical entertainment" featuring the first lady. The same argument was made when Ike's sixty-sixth birthday, held at the Statler Hotel, was celebrated via a television party. Actor James Stewart served as on-air host, and actresses Helen Hayes and Irene Dunne were on hand to cut the cake. Ike and Mamie watched from the White House, but the two, along with John, Barbara, and the grandchildren, appeared on camera in a feature during the celebration. *New York Times* critic Jack Gould said the party reminded him of the show *This Is Your Life,* but the event, along with the earlier party for Mamie, took a new road in bringing a candidate before the public. The vote-for-me message was implicit, rather than the usual direct campaign ads.[16]

The first lady's popularity was used to garner votes, and, intended or not, so too were the grandchildren. John bristled and called it a "gimmick" when son David (who was home with his sisters) was made an "honorary chairman" of the Republican National Convention. The use of a candidate's children and/or grandchildren had not reached the level of late twentieth-century politicking, which accepted, even required, their presence on podiums, before TV cameras, and in advertisements. Nevertheless, the Eisenhower children were a known entity. During Eisenhower's first term, the grandchildren had been the subject of newspaper and magazine articles, and their grandparents' obvious pleasure in their company added another reason to "like" Ike.[17]

A downside to the children's visibility was their exploitation by those opposed to the administration and its handling of public policies. This was especially true after the 1954 U.S. Supreme Court ruling in *Brown v. Board of Education,* which determined that "separate but equal" school segregation of black and white students was

Ike, Mamie, Richard and Pat Nixon on election eve, 1956. National Park Service Photograph by Abbie Rowe, Courtesy Dwight D. Eisenhower Presidential Library

unconstitutional. The president received outraged letters asking about the status of his grandchildren's enrollment. Some accused the Eisenhower administration of forcing integration on ordinary citizens while those at the highest rungs of government kept their children in segregated schools. The accusations were encouraged by stories in southern newspapers that focused on where the Eisenhower children were being educated. In fact, David and Anne were in a private school; Susan attended an integrated kindergarten; and all the children went to an integrated Sunday school. Election issues of 1956 were not just about integration, but the intense emotions of voters reached beyond the president to his family.[18]

In October and November 1956, President Eisenhower curtailed campaigning to deal with two major international crises—one in the Middle East, the other in Hungary. His distance from the campaign trail did not impact the outcome. Eisenhower received 57.8 percent of the popular vote and carried forty-one states. He and Mamie had another four years in the White House, and because January 20, 1957, fell on a Sunday, there were two inauguration ceremonies. The first, on Sunday, was a private event in the White House, attended by the Eisenhowers, the Nixons, and a few family members. The next day, the public ceremony took place.

The first lady continued to perform her many White House duties, and she kept up a schedule of appearances for charity events, White House tours, and public functions. After the home at Gettysburg was completed, she and Ike spent time at the farm. There were also visits to Camp David and Newport, Rhode Island. Behind the scenes, no matter where they were, Mamie's worries over her husband's health were constant. She routinely reported Ike's current condition to Dr. Snyder. If Ike had a headache, the doctor heard about it. If the blood vessels stood out on Ike's forehead, the doctor was told. Even ordinary details, such as when Ike went to bed and how he slept, were passed on. She worried when he forgot to wear a hat out in the sun, and decided that someone besides Ike should tie his shoes because it might be a strain when he leaned over. She took no chances when it came to Ike's health and could firmly get her way if the situation demanded. When the president suffered a slight stroke in November 1957, he decided, after a few hours of rest, that he could attend a White House dinner being given for King Mohammed V of Morocco. The doctor opposed it. So did Mamie, telling her husband that if he insisted on attending, she would not. Ike went back to bed. Mamie hosted the dinner, with Vice President Nixon standing in for the president. It was a good example of the strong personality that otherwise appeared rather frivolous with those fashionable hats and her love of pink. "Mrs. Eisenhower is infinitely feminine," noted *Newsweek* in 1960. "But," continued the magazine, "she has a will before which any general would retreat. The President's famous temper holds no terrors for her." When Mamie disagreed with Ike, she could be abrupt, but she was just as apt to "smooth out Ike's occasional irritability" with her "gay laugh and personality." That was the way Virginia Conner saw the Ike and Mamie relationship all those years ago in Panama. Mamie was a "very, very strong" woman, said Nancy Reagan, who met Mrs. Eisenhower in Palm Desert, where her parents socialized with the Eisenhowers, and, said Mrs. Reagan, Mamie could exert "power over Ike."[19]

How much power Mamie had in certain instances is a point of conjecture. Ike's participation in Richard Nixon's campaign for president in 1960 is a good example. In his memoir *Waging Peace,* Eisenhower wrote of his "high regard" for Nixon and his hopes that his vice president would run for president in 1960. Privately, the president conveyed the same message. In his birthday greeting to Pat Nixon, for example, he wrote: "You know that I hope this year of 1960 will bring you and Dick everything that you want and so richly deserve." Ike's health, however, became an issue during Nixon's presidential bid, at least for Mamie. She went behind Ike's back and asked Pat to pass the word that she was worried about Ike's health and the physical strain of making numerous speeches. Eisenhower's participation had to be limited. As a result, the Nixon campaign did not accept Ike's offer to add more states to his schedule of appearances. Of this episode, Susan Eisenhower writes that "family members are divided on how much influence Mamie really had, and whether her concern stopped Nixon from asking Ike for assistance." Some in the family, including Milton Eisenhower, contended that the Nixon campaign did not want to be seen as "dependent on the President's great popularity" and asked Ike to make only a few speeches. Mamie had nothing to do with the decision. Nevertheless, Mamie did try to intercede by telling Pat Nixon of her concerns.[20]

Mamie's reports to Dr. Snyder and her fussing over things like Ike wearing hats or eating a salt-free diet had their price. Being watched irritated Ike, and like other couples in similar situations, there were periods of tension when Ike felt that not only his doctors but his anxious wife spent too much time trying to control his everyday activities. On one occasion, he decided to leave for a trip earlier than planned, despite a bad cold, and Mamie "immediately took exception to it and tried to persuade him to delay the departure." The president angrily agreed, stormed into his dressing room, and spent the remainder of the afternoon there. Dr. Snyder, who witnessed the scene, wrote that Ike "would have no part of Mamie," who was worried that Ike's anger would induce another stroke.[21]

Despite the shaky moments, the two truly cared about each other. They were openly affectionate, holding hands and exchanging good-bye kisses. Mamie worked to keep romance in the marriage. "She keeps about herself an aura of special femininity that makes her an object to be courted all her life," noted Vivian Cadden for *McCall's* magazine. The couple marked each wedding anniversary, but in 1959 the celebration was unusually special. They repeated their vows on their forty-third anniversary. There was an informal get-together with members of the White House executive staff and their wives in the family quarters. Then Ike announced that the rest of the evening belonged to the Eisenhowers, General and Mrs. Leonard Heaton (Ike's surgeon), and Mr. and Mrs. Neil H. McElroy (secretary of defense). All were celebrating wedding anniversaries, and all repeated their vows before a minister in the East Room. Asked his formula for a successful marriage, Ike replied: "No, I haven't any formula. I can just say that it's been a very happy experience. . . . a successful marriage I think gets happier as the years go by." The marriage had endured some bumpy periods, and both Ike and Mamie were strong-willed people. Had the marriage ever been in jeopardy? Barbara Walters asked the question in her last interview with the former first lady. Mamie's first response was a look that seemed to register impatience with the question. "All marriages are in jeopardy," Mamie instructed. "That's where your good sense comes in." As for the possibility that there had been another woman, namely, Kay Summersby, Mamie was firm: "I wouldn't have stayed with him five minutes if I hadn't had the greatest respect in the world for him, and I never lost my respect."[22]

As the time ticked down on the Eisenhowers' stay in the White House, Mamie continued to answer her voluminous mail. By inclination, Mamie was a letter writer, and the habit was reinforced by her years in a military culture that expected the courtesies of congratulatory letters for promotions or acknowledging someone's thoughtfulness for remembering birthdays or anniversaries. During her many travels and postings with Ike, Mamie regularly wrote to her parents, whom she often addressed as the "folksies." She also corresponded with friends and army acquaintances on a regular basis. As first lady, Mamie continued to write to friends and family, and she wrote to those whom she no longer saw but who had been important at some point in her life. She corresponded, for instance, with the woman who, as a sixteen-year-old, had been her Sunday

Mamie works at her letter writing during the 1952 campaign.
Dwight D. Eisenhower Presidential Library

school teacher, and she had a recurring correspondence with Mary Newton, who had worked for Mrs. Eisenhower during the war. While Mamie was in the White House, Newton sometimes talked with Mamie by phone, and long after the Eisenhowers retired to private life, she continued to send letters and birthday greetings to her former employer. While in the White House, Mamie Eisenhower became, said one historian, a "pen pal" with the American people.[23]

The war years gave Mamie her first brush with notoriety and the experience of receiving mail from people she did not know. That mail became a deluge after Ike's nomination and election in 1952. It astounded her. Between the election and inauguration, she received at least 1,000 letters per day. She was "determined to answer each one in a personal way," but the sheer volume meant that she could only sign most. It was an accomplishment just to do that. To a friend she wrote, "I am swamped with mail. Poor Mrs. McCaffree stays up until all hours of the night, typing these notes of mine." Of course, Mrs. McCaffree had the assistance of a secretarial pool, and form letters were developed for a number of circumstances. Still, Mamie dictated as many as possible, providing that personal touch. "You always write as if you meant it," Senator Stuart Symington told her. "That is one of the reasons you have the country in the palm of your hand." No one commented on, or seemed to notice, that in an era when few married women continued to use their maiden names in some fashion, Mamie always signed her letters "Mamie Doud Eisenhower."[24]

While she lived in the White House, Mamie's mail fluctuated between 250 and 400 pieces per day. The mail varied widely in content. Some people asked for some sort of aid. About 300 requests per week asked for a signed picture and/or autograph. Strangers wrote offering advice, or asking for it. Others sent words of support or prayers. Each letter was acknowledged, and Mamie particularly appreciated the thoughtfulness of those who remembered her on special occasions. When the Nixons' daughters sent Mamie drawings for her birthday in 1954, she asked Pat to "please give them a kiss for me." To the girls she wrote individual thank-you notes. "[Julie] I just loved the birthday cake you drew" and "[Tricia] I just loved the little [cutout] windows in it and peeked through each one." Mrs. Nixon always sent the first lady a birthday gift, and in 1957, she and the wives of cabinet members gave Mamie a Limoges box. Mrs. Eisenhower wrote, thanking "dear Pat for this extra special gift."[25]

Seasonal events increased the mail volume. In a letter to a friend, Mamie reported that she was "relaxing" by signing "hundreds of graduation letters and autograph cards." Christmas brought about 700 pieces of mail each day. Some asked for help, such as having gifts for their children, but the bulk contained greeting cards from wellwishers. Holiday cards also were sent out by the White House, and these deserve some notice, since they are said to represent "a unique collection of Christmas cards unlike those of any other Presidential era." All were created as a result of Ike meeting Joyce C. Hall, chief executive of Hallmark, in 1950 when Hall was asked to serve on a committee that was raising funds to build a museum to General Eisenhower in Abilene, Kansas. For each Christmas that the Eisenhowers were in the White House, Hallmark created four types of cards. There was the commemorative card, printed in limited edition and featuring one of Eisenhower's own paintings, and there was the official White House Christmas card. Between 1953 and 1960, the number receiving this card almost tripled from just over 1,000 to over 3,000. Additionally, the Eisenhowers had a personal card for friends and family; in 1957, for example, a caricature of Ike and Mamie in a golf cart adorned the front, and in 1958, the image was the Eisenhower Museum in Abilene. The last type of card, which Mamie "adored," was the "Mamie Bangs" card. Created as "an affectionate holiday greeting for close personal friends," each card in the yearly series carried a playful caricature of Mamie and her bangs.[26]

At no time was the amount of mail more voluminous or Mamie's intent to respond more pronounced than when Ike suffered his heart attack in 1955. Hundreds of letters expressing concern and offering prayers arrived. Mamie was determined to answer each one. "At the time I thought she was out of her mind," said John Eisenhower, "but somehow over the weeks she was successful. Doubtless, it proved excellent therapy for her own spirits to have something, no matter how overwhelming, to do." To friends she wrote personal notes, and the short form letter sent to acknowledge the thoughtfulness of wellwishers had Mamie's touch. She signed each letter. "People are marveling that you have personally signed so much mail," Pat Nixon told her. "They are filled with admiration and appreciation." A case in point was the owner of a delicatessen in the Nixons' neighborhood. He told Mrs. Nixon "in great detail" about the letter a friend had received from Mamie. To Pat's own letter of concern for Ike's health, Mamie replied: "The President was as deeply touched as I when I read him your kind letter, and joins me in sending you and Dick warm appreciation for this further example of the way you have brightened our spirits during this time of anxiety."[27]

During her eight years in the White House, Mamie Eisenhower responded to at least 500,000 letters and cards, and during the post–White House years, strangers still wrote to her, as if she was the friend next door. In one instance a woman listed a string of family misfortunes and asked for clothing; Mamie responded with a box of clothes for the family. Oftentimes, letter writers asked for advice. To those young people who wrote that they wanted to "make the world a better place," to do something constructive, Mamie invariably suggested that they contact People to People. It was an organization established during Ike's administration because he believed that divisiveness and conflict could be countered when people from many cultures and backgrounds met one another on a personal basis.[28]

Over a lifetime of letter writing, Mamie's correspondence carried her personal imprint. Her writing voice suited the occasion. To the daughters of White House usher J. B. West, her thank-you note for homemade cookies was warmly appreciative: "Even though it was right after breakfast when your daddy brought them to me, I had to open your box—and naturally I ate one of the cookies immediately!" Mamie's letters were sometimes newsy, often humorous, and invariably caring. As when she wrote Pat Nixon a short note wishing her "an enjoyable" summer vacation, Mamie Eisenhower took the time to let others know that she was thinking of them. When she received mail, she felt obligated to acknowledge the sender. She once told an interviewer: "If anyone takes the time to go buy a card, to address it, put it into an envelope, seal it and put a stamp on it, the least I can do is thank them."[29]

Arriving in the White House mail were requests for help in raising funds for some project such as building a new church or modernizing a school. The custom in these cases, begun during the Wilson administration, was to send a steel engraving of the White House, which could be used by the recipients for fund-raising. There were also requests for monetary contributions to one cause or another. Generally, these were answered with a polite letter saying the Mrs. Eisenhower received so many requests that it was impossible for her to grant each one. Many other letters, however, were answered with a donation. Generally, the amount was not large. Five to ten dollars was the norm. How Mamie decided which requests received donations was not explained in her correspondence, but the recipients represented an interesting cross section of good causes. Contributions, for example, went to a prison chaplain; a home for unwed mothers in Maryland; Legal Aid in New York; the Boys' Athletic

League; Madison Square Boys' Club; the March of Dimes; the Washington, D.C., Community Chest; and the historical society in Nutley, New York, which wanted to preserve an old schoolhouse.[30]

During Christmas season, the White House was flooded with letters from parents who were unable to afford presents for their children. Mamie told the staff to "dip into the toy room," a large storage closet filled with gifts sent to the Eisenhower grandchildren. A large number of the items came from toy manufacturer Louis Marx. From this cache of toys, the staff was instructed to "supply as many requests as we could fill." Toys and games also went to charities that housed children or conducted programs for them. Among those requesting, and receiving, toys were the Christ Child Farm for Convalescent Children in Rockville, Maryland, and the Manhattanville Community Center in New York. On at least one occasion donated television sets were sent to institutions that worked with delinquent or dependent children, homes for the aged, and a place that was described as a "Negro Settlement House" in Washington, D.C., that was "very worthy" but received "very few gifts."[31]

For a number of charities and worthwhile organizations, the first lady not only gave contributions but also lent her name and presence. She was honorary president of the Girl Scouts; sponsor of the annual Easter Seal appeal for crippled children and adults; and a visible supporter of fund drives for United Cerebral Palsy and the New York Association for the Blind. During her first four years in the White House, she launched as many as five charity drives a week, and she continued to lend her name to charitable causes and organizations during the second term. Visibly supporting charitable projects has long been a role expected of first ladies, while charities and good causes rely upon the participation of first ladies to raise public awareness. Mrs. Eisenhower appeared for well-known causes, such as the Girl Scouts and Easter Seals, but in the same no-favoritism mode that she employed for the press, she also lent her name to lesser-known organizations. Many of these were in some way associated with health care. Besides appearing for organizations working with crippled children, the blind, and the physically or mentally impaired, Mrs. Eisenhower gave her time and position to more than fifteen health and medical research foundations, including the

American Heart Association. Her support for that organization began in 1953, but after Ike's heart attack, the AHA received focused attention. She became the national honorary chair of the 1957 "Heart Campaign," and through her visible involvement, the association saw the number of its volunteers dramatically rise and its donations increase by 70 percent.[32]

As part of her work for various causes, Mrs. Eisenhower also made public service announcements; this was in contrast to Bess Truman's rare statements that encouraged people to buy U.S. savings bonds or to contribute to the March of Dimes. A number of Mamie's announcements were released for the print media. Others were used for radio and television broadcasts. The American Cancer Society, U.S. savings bonds, United Nations Week, and the USO all received attention. So did the American Red Cross, for which Mamie had volunteered as a military wife, and Federal Civil Defense. The messages for the Red Cross and Civil Defense were especially intended for the women of America. While women went about their daily lives, said the Civil Defense message, they should never forget about the cold war and the threat of the atomic bomb. As upsetting as it might be, "We Americans are asked today to face the grim facts that the women of the nation, of all ages, from girls to grandmothers, must do our part in Civil Defense." The federal agency offered informational materials that outlined steps for preparing emergency kits, as well as tips for readying the household for disasters. And, both parents and classroom teachers were encouraged to teach children what to do in case of a nuclear attack—"duck and cover." (Although the service announcement did not mention it, White House staff and residents drilled, too, taking cover in an underground shelter.) The appeal to mothers also took center stage when the topic was blood donation to the Red Cross during the Korean War. "The Mothers of this country know today that every pint of blood contributed may mean life to a wounded son in Korea," read Mamie's announcement. In this instance, and in others, statements connected with the sentiment that "mothers respond to any call which promises greater protection and happiness for their families."[33]

Within the White House, Mamie had her own causes. She would have preferred to renovate the Executive Mansion, but money was lacking. Certainly, she was no different from other first ladies who

One of Mamie's many charitable causes was the American Heart Association. Pictured with the first lady is the 1959 poster child for the Heart Fund, the president of the American Heart Association, and the chairman of the National Heart Campaign. National Park Service Photograph by Abbie Rowe, Courtesy Dwight D. Eisenhower Presidential Library

had their own ideas about style and taste. After Bess Truman toured Mamie through the White House, for example, she told the staff to look forward to "plenty of pink." It hardly would have been Mrs. Truman's decorating choice, but Mamie loved it. Mamie responded in much the same way, but with more disapproval, after touring Mrs. Kennedy through the Executive Mansion. She told the staff,

"She's planning to redo every room in this house. . . . There certainly are going to be some changes made around here!" This was not so much a statement of partisanship aimed at a Democrat coming into the White House as a reproach of what Mrs. Kennedy had in mind. As a former first lady, Mrs. Eisenhower was much more supportive of the changes made to the Executive Mansion by Pat Nixon than by Jacqueline Kennedy. In fact, said a longtime White House insider, when Mamie visited the White House during the Johnson and Nixon administrations, she never failed to ask, "How did you ever let that woman [Mrs. Kennedy] ruin that beautiful chandelier?" The object in question was a silver chandelier installed in the State Dining Room in 1902 and gilded under Jacqueline's renovation plan.[34]

Since Mrs. Eisenhower had no budget to do the sort of extensive rework that she would have liked to accomplish, she took on several smaller projects. Some furniture was restored for the Lincoln bedroom, and a portrait of Mary Todd Lincoln was added. Items from former presidents Herbert Hoover and James Monroe were taken out of storage and appropriately placed, and she completed the White House collection of presidential china. Presidents Jackson, Taft, Harding, Coolidge, and Hoover were not represented in the collection because they had no official state china. Mamie felt that "since several other presidents were represented by their personal china . . . the collection would be enhanced" by adding the family china of those presidents not represented. She worked with a curator from the Smithsonian Institution to locate and secure the pieces. (It was not until Jacqueline Kennedy began her White House renovation that the White House had a staff position of curator.) Mamie's project was completed in 1959, and the collection was displayed in what is now known as the China Room. Later, when the Smithsonian published a book on the subject, Mamie provided the introduction. Adjacent to the China Room was the Gold Room. The collection of gold plates, goblets, vases, and bowls was begun by President Monroe and added to by later first families. In 1956, Margaret Thompson Biddle, a close friend of Mamie's, bequeathed her collection of more than 1,500 vermeil pieces, made in Europe between 1700 and 1900, to the existing collection. Both the vermeil and the china acquisitions were important additions to the Executive Mansion, but Mamie's approach to

Mamie in the White House China Room; one of Mrs. Eisenhower's White House projects was completing the collection of presidential china. National Park Service Photograph by Abbie Rowe, Courtesy Dwight D. Eisenhower Presidential Library

renovating the Diplomatic Reception Room was distinctively innovative. For the first time, a first lady decorated a room in antique furniture paid for by an outside organization. This was a precursor to the Kennedy approach to using private donations in redoing the White House, and in this case, the National Association of Interior Designers provided the support and expertise for the room that was completed shortly before the Eisenhowers left the White House.[35]

Despite her additions to the Executive Mansion and the number of causes and worthwhile organizations Mamie Eisenhower supported, she did not receive widespread public recognition for her efforts. This was partly a result of little concentrated focus on one area or subject. Lack of media coverage was also a factor. Mamie Eisenhower's tenure in the White House, in fact, represented a dividing line in the way that first ladies approached the role of spokeswoman and/or activist. Among earlier first ladies of the twentieth century, Lou Hoover and Eleanor Roosevelt were known champions of specific causes, but there was no public expectation that first ladies have a "project." Jacqueline Kennedy's White House renovation and Lady Bird Johnson's environmental/beautification projects changed that. No first lady who came after could be without her cause. In the first weeks of becoming first lady, for instance, Pat Nixon was pressured by the media to announce her "focus," her issue. The administration decided that her project would encourage volunteerism in civic and public life. Mrs. Nixon firmly believed in the value of volunteerism, but she would have preferred to be defined by what she considered to be her most significant work—personal diplomacy, which began during the Eisenhower years when she made "goodwill" trips to fifty-three countries and which she hoped to continue as first lady.[36]

In regard to projects, the role for first lady altered after Mamie Eisenhower's years in the White House. Later first ladies were expected to have a specific issue or cause. Some proved to be more memorable or influential than others, but for better or worse, first ladies could no longer take the Mamie-like approach of speaking for many causes or having several projects. It was a change that Mamie herself noted in 1977 when she told Rosalynn Carter: "I stayed busy all the time and loved being in the White House, but I was never expected to do all the things you have to do." Mamie did not give herself enough credit. Her efforts produced noticeable results in a number of areas, but her work was not widely recognized by the press or the public. Certainly, there was never any idea of creating a public image based on one defined project. If anything, the lack of press and public recognition provided a lesson to future first ladies who were increasingly aware of image shaped by the causes they endorsed and how those causes defined them to the public.[37]

* * *

In the waning months of 1960, Mamie Eisenhower was ready to relinquish the duties of first lady, and she looked forward to the couple's move to the Gettysburg farm, where most of the family's personal possessions were already in place. The transition to her new home would not be difficult. Rather than feeling sad about leaving the Executive Mansion and her role there, she felt sentimental. Being in the White House and carrying out her role of first lady made her feel that she was "a part of history." Social occasions began to take on an aura of finality. A luncheon for presswomen "was in the nature of a farewell." One reporter noted that the first lady's eyes "glistened with tears." And, as Mamie said good-bye to guests attending her nieces' social debut at the White House in November 1960, she was heard to say to more than one friend, "I guess this is the last time I'll see you here."[38]

On the day of John F. Kennedy's inauguration, the Eisenhowers slipped away after the swearing-in ceremonies. They attended a postinaugural luncheon with friends and members of Ike's administration, allowing them time to reminiscence. Then, leaving Washington for Gettysburg, Ike and Mamie "made a fantastic discovery." They were now private citizens. "We were free," said Ike. Mamie frankly admitted to a journalist that she would be "perfectly satisfied to be known as a housewife." She had continued to carry out her public roles, but the last four years in the Executive Mansion had been difficult. Mamie's concerns for Ike's health had affected her own in small ways, and in 1960 she was devastated by the death of her mother. The couple was ready to retire to their farm. John and Barbara had moved nearby in the late 1950s, and Mamie anticipated that she and Ike would "always have them near us." Once the Eisenhowers were settled into their home, their days took on a routine. Ike went to an office in Gettysburg to work on his memoirs. Mamie ran the house, and the couple often entertained. "Life went on very much the same," said Mamie. "In fact I think it was a little bit better, because we were home and our own people were around us."[39]

The years of retirement were not all spent at Gettysburg. The Eisenhowers continued to vacation at "Mamie's Cabin," built for their use by the membership of Augusta National Golf Club. They took a trip to Europe in 1962, bringing along their grandchildren David

Ike and Mamie at their Gettysburg home. National Park Service Photograph by
Abbie Rowe, Courtesy Dwight D. Eisenhower Presidential Library

and Anne and visiting many heads of state and dignitaries they had
come to regard as friends. In the United States, the Eisenhowers
sometimes lived in a home at the Eldorado Golf Club in Palm
Desert, California, and while Ike worked on his memoirs, he used an
office at the nearby ranch of Jacqueline Cochran. There were trips to
Boone, Iowa, and to Abilene, Kansas. Mamie donated items to her
birthplace, which was being restored in Boone, and both Eisenhowers were actively involved in the completion of the museum, exhibits, and library in Abilene. They also worked tirelessly for Eisenhower College, a small liberal arts school in Seneca Falls, New York.
Dedicated in 1965, the school was the sort of small college that Ike
once pictured for himself as a college president. He wrote Ann
Whitman that he was so dedicated to the school's success that he
would "do almost anything to further the project." Mamie felt the
same way. She sold her Chrysler to raise money and penned an article for *Reader's Digest* to advance the school's visibility. She served
on the school's board of directors, as well as the board of two other
colleges. The Eisenhowers' best efforts could not, however, assure

the school's success. In 1979 the college was acquired by the Rochester Institute of Technology. The last class graduated in 1983, and the property was later acquired by New York Chiropractic College.[40]

Mamie's postpresidential causes also included serving as cochair in the fund-raising efforts to build the National Cultural Center, now known as the Kennedy Center for the Performing Arts. As early as 1955, President Eisenhower had expressed an interest in having a "public building for the arts" in Washington, D.C., and in 1958 he signed legislation to create the National Cultural Center. The enabling bill stipulated that the center had to be self-sustaining and privately funded, but it was not until the Kennedy administration that the first large national fund-raising campaign began. In November 1962, there was a $100-a-plate gala dinner with well-known performers providing the entertainment. The event was broadcast by closed-circuit television to fund-raising groups around the country, and Ike and Mamie appeared via hookup from Augusta, Georgia. The next year, Mamie served as honorary cochair with Jacqueline Kennedy for a fund-raising dinner in New York City. Mamie was especially interested in the success of the center, one of the projects initiated during the Eisenhower administration.[41]

The couple's activities and travels were curtailed when Ike had a heart attack in November 1965. Realizing that another might be fatal, he and Mamie gave the Gettysburg farm to the Department of the Interior to be administered by the National Park Service as a museum after Ike and Mamie were gone. He went to Denver and arranged to have Ikky's coffin moved from Fairmount Cemetery for reburial at the Place of Meditation on the grounds of the Eisenhower Presidential Library and Museum in Abilene. He and Mamie also planned to be buried in the nondenominational Place of Meditation.[42]

In March 1968, there was another heart attack. This one placed Ike at Walter Reed Army Hospital for the remainder of his life. Mamie had a small room next to his. On the rare occasions that she went to Gettysburg, she told a friend, "[I] miss my beau terribly." As in earlier hospital stays, she monitored the number of visitors and the length of visits and kept upsetting news of current events from reaching Ike. She also visited soldiers in the hospital wards, as she had done when Ike was hospitalized in 1965. These combat veterans of Vietnam seemed "so young—so very young. Too young to be hurt." They brought to mind other soldiers and another war in which Ike was the Supreme Allied Commander in Europe. Mamie later said that during this time at Walter Reed, she thought about the responsibilities Ike carried during World War II. "I often wondered how in the world he could ever go to sleep at night with all those horrors that he had seen [during the war] years, those awful [concentration] camps, and the responsibilities of so many lives."[43]

As time neared for the August 1968 Republican National Convention, Ike broke his policy of staying out of primary and convention infighting and insisted on addressing the assembly to endorse Richard Nixon. Mamie did not interfere, but as television cameras were set up in the hospital ward, she knew that the speech would be a tremendous strain on her husband. Her fears proved true. The next day he suffered another heart attack. In the months that followed, he would rally, visit with family, and then have a setback. He died on March 28, 1969. Mamie was with him, holding his hand. "I am sad but grateful that the General was so clear in mind right to the end," she wrote Ann Whitman. "I held his hand until he was gone." It was the most difficult thing she had ever done, but as she told an interviewer in 1972, "I think I've turned out to be much stronger than I thought I ever could be."[44]

After a funeral service at the National Cathedral in Washington attended by world leaders and royalty, the casket was taken by train to Abilene. Thousands of people lined the route, and Mamie watched the line as it stretched mile after mile into the night. Ike was laid to rest next to Ikky. Mamie said, "I did not feel badly leaving my husband at the little Chapel in Abilene because he is just across the street from his boyhood home." Mrs. Eisenhower returned to Abilene on several occasions to visit the grave site and once expressed the sentiment, "I am glad that my memories of Ike are of a very attractive Lieutenant, for to me he never grew old." He would always be her beau, and she, his sweetheart.[45]

During her years alone, Mamie continued to live at the Gettysburg farm. Beginning in 1965, former first ladies had Secret Service protection, somewhat easing her family's concerns when John went to Belgium as American ambassador. She visited John and his family in Brussels, and back in the States, she continued to travel to her favorite places. She also appeared at events commemorating Ike. She attended the opening of the Eisenhower Medical Center in Palm Desert, California, the dedication of Eisenhower Hall at West Point, the dedication of the Eisenhower Theater at the Kennedy Center for the Performing Arts, and the dedication of the Eisenhower Corridor at the Pentagon, and she was present for the launch of the USS *Eisenhower*.

She was a frequent guest in the Nixon White House, where, recalled Julie Nixon Eisenhower, "No matter how busy my mother's schedule, when Mamie visited, she always set aside time for what Mamie relished most, 'girl talk.'" Mamie thought Pat "a wonderful woman," and while Mamie was first lady, she considered Pat "my helpmate. . . . The Rock of Gibraltar." The comments clash with such apocryphal stories as that told by one writer who said that when Mollie Parnis asked Mamie about doing some clothes for Mrs. Nixon, Mamie dismissed the idea by responding, "Let the poor thing go to Garfinckel's [department store] and buy off the rack." In fact, the prevailing assumption among many historians that Nixon felt ill-used by President Eisenhower colors the general perception of the Mamie-Pat relationship. A good argument can be made to counter the idea that Eisenhower and Nixon lacked a good working relationship. As for Mrs. Eisenhower and Mrs. Nixon, documentary evidence and family accounts demonstrate that the two developed a good personal friendship that grew out of their public responsibilities. Within days of the 1953 inauguration, the private residence that Mamie guarded so carefully was open to the vice president's wife, and Mamie broke with tradition by inviting the Nixons to accompany her and Ike in the receiving line when the Eisenhowers hosted their first diplomatic reception. In January 1954, Ike and Mamie gave a formal dinner party in honor of the Nixons, and as the eighty invited guests moved through the receiving line, Mamie introduced the Nixons "as two of their best friends."[46]

During her eight years in the White House, Mamie relied on Pat Nixon to take her place at a scheduled appearance or social occasion, and on a personal note, the two visited privately in the White House. After the Nixons moved into their new home, a thirty-year-old English Tudor that Pat loved, the Eisenhowers accepted an invitation to dinner. On the surface, one dinner in the Nixon's home may seem a trivial event, but in the context of understanding that the Eisenhowers seldom visited private homes, the evening takes on additional meaning. If nothing else, Mamie understood how important it was to Pat to show off the house to Mamie and the president. Publicly, Mamie and Pat were seen together at charity fashion shows, senate wives' luncheons, and somber occasions such as the 1958 State of the Union address, when Mamie invited Pat to sit with her. After leaving the White House, Mamie felt that both the Nixons had been loyal to her and Ike, and she returned the friendship and loyalty during their darkest times. After it became apparent during the Watergate scandal that Nixon would resign, Mamie wrote: "Dearest Pat, I only want to say I'm thinking of you today—always you will have my warm affection as will your husband President Nixon—Your friend."[47]

As a former first lady, Mamie Eisenhower continued to do the things that she did best. She valued her friends and treasured her family. She continued to take an interest in a variety of causes, without making noticeable headlines. She was no different from how she had been as first lady. To that role she brought many talents, as well as an approach and mind-set that were shaped by the many years of being an army wife. In retirement, Mrs. Eisenhower did not think of her legacy as first lady. She simply hoped that people might remember her as a friend.

In the years since Mamie Eisenhower's residence in the White House, the general attitude among writers has been to dismiss her as an aged grandmother who offered little to the position of first lady. It has been common, for instance, to suggest that while she was more involved in the responsibilities of first lady than her immediate predecessor, Bess Truman, she was not as glamorous or socially sophisticated as her successor, Jacqueline Kennedy. The assertion that Mrs. Kennedy overshadowed Mrs. Eisenhower in bringing sparkle to the White House and personal fashion is not, however, an accurate assessment of Mamie Eisenhower's private or public White House persona.

Rather than belabor who had more style, it is important to recognize that social and political consciousness of a time period changes perceptions of a first lady. Mamie Eisenhower was a perfect fit for the 1950s, but not for the latter twentieth century. The new women's movement, which by the 1970s had brought significant changes to social thinking and behavior, cast Mamie, the self-proclaimed

The former first lady at the Eisenhower Presidential Museum in 1973; she stands
next to an exhibit of her wedding dress and portrait.
Staff Photo, Dwight D. Eisenhower Presidential Library

homemaker, in a negative light. The movement's context stressed
total equality at home and in the workplace. Being a less visible partner was equivalent to sexual inequality, and Mamie's ideas about
marriage as a partnership in which each party had separate responsibilities seemed hopelessly traditional. Mamie, who privately had
definite opinions of her own and who felt herself an equal partner
in Ike's military career and White House years, had never pushed

herself forward as a first lady. To observers, she was the traditional wife—although a closer look at the Eisenhower marriage would have revealed a few nontraditional role reversals. Ike cooked and gardened. Mamie did not, but she handled the family's finances. The first lady was, however, remembered for what she did not do, rather than for what she did. She had not labeled herself as an equal to her husband by actively speaking out on social issues or policies. She did not champion any grand cause or agenda. She certainly never sat in on cabinet meetings or discussions of policy. Her media image, so in tune with the popular culture of the fifties, did not translate well into the late twentieth century.

For the era of the 1950s, Mamie Eisenhower instinctively seemed to understand the mood of the people and what they expected of her as first lady. Despite the ways in which Mamie has been evaluated, or ignored, her popularity with the public remained after she left the White House. Her name first appeared on *Good Housekeeping* magazine's annual poll of the world's ten most admired women in 1952, when Ike was elected, and she continued to appear on the list every year long after she left the White House. In 1969 and 1970, with the memory of Ike's death fresh in the minds of Americans, Mamie's name moved to first place on the list. In the same years, Pat Nixon was listed at third and second place, respectively; Jacqueline Kennedy was at fifth both years; and Lady Bird Johnson placed at sixth and eighth, respectively. Considering that Mrs. Eisenhower was seldom in the news during the postpresidential years, her appearance on the list year after year suggests that the public felt an affinity with the woman who seemed very much like them. The instant connection between Mamie and the public, first noted during the 1952 campaign, remained intact.[48]

Mamie suffered a stroke on September 25, 1979. Her family had realized for some time that her health was failing. She knew it, too, and being the well-organized woman that she was, she kept a bag packed—just in case she had to be rushed to the hospital. She also prepared a garment bag with the dress in which she wanted to be buried—the evening gown worn on her fiftieth wedding anniversary. A little over a month after her stroke, Mamie Doud Eisenhower died on November 1. After a service at Fort Myer, attended by President and Mrs. Jimmy Carter and other dignitaries, Mamie's body was brought to Abilene, where she was buried beside Ike and their son Doud Dwight at the Place of Meditation.[49]

Among the obituaries and commentaries that followed Mamie's death, that of Marian Christy, writing for the *Boston Globe,* captured Mamie's character, the way she lived her life, and her approach to being first lady of the land: "There are very few originals in the world. And when one leaves it there is a void. Mamie Eisenhower was an original. She had the courage to define herself rather than have outsiders tell her who she was and what she should be. . . . She set an image for the role of the classic wife, the classic mother, the classic non-political President's wife. She had the guts to be her classic self. She was 'Mamie.' "[50]

NOTES

ABBREVIATIONS

BE Papers	Barbara Eisenhower Papers, 1892–1976
Bookman Papers	George Bookman Papers, 1981–1993
Cochran Papers	Jacqueline Cochran Papers, 1932–1975
DDE	Dwight David Eisenhower
E. Corres. Series, Gruenther Papers	Eisenhower Correspondence Series, Alfred M. Gruenther Papers, 1941–1983
EL	Eisenhower Presidential Library, Abilene, Kansas
Mattingly Papers	Col. [Dr.] Thomas W. Mattingly Papers
McCaffree Papers	Mary Jane McCaffree Papers
MDE	Mamie Doud Eisenhower
MDE Centennial	Mamie Doud Eisenhower Centennial, video
MDE Papers	Mamie Doud Eisenhower Papers
Nixon Library	Richard Nixon Library and Birthplace, Yorba Linda, California
PPF, Central Files	Presidential Personal File, Central Files
Snyder Papers	Dr. Howard McCrum Snyder Papers, 1931–1955
Sullivan Papers	Wallace Sullivan Papers, 1931–1955
White House Social Office	White House Social Office Records, 1953–1961
White House Social Office, Tolley	White House Social Office, A. B. Tolley Records, 1952–1961
Whitman Papers	Ann C. Whitman Personal Papers
Wyden Papers	Barbara Wyden Papers, 1944–1945

THE MILITARY LIFE

1. MDE, interview with Barbara Walters, ABC, *20/20,* Nov. 1, 1979, video, EL; David Eisenhower, Eisenhower family interviews, video, Presidential Gallery, museum, EL.

2. MDE, oral history interview, July–Aug., 1972, transcript, 117, EL; Lydia Spencer Lane, *I Married a Soldier, or Old Days in the Old Army* (Philadelphia: Lippincott, 1893; reprint, Albuquerque, NM: Horn and Wallace, 1964), introduction, 10.

3. MDE oral history, 149, EL; "Message from Mrs. Eisenhower to Editors Attending Press Week, January 5, 1952," box 35, press requests file (1), MDE Papers, White House Series, EL; MDE to Douds, Sept. 1940, box 3, family letters 1940 file (3), BE Papers, EL; Susan Eisenhower, *Mrs. Ike: Memories and Reflections on the Life of Mamie Eisenhower* (New York: Farrar, Straus and Giroux, 1996), 63.

4. Eisenhower, *Mrs. Ike,* 9, 12. Mrs. Doud's name also has been spelled "Elvira"; I have used "Elivera," since it appears that way in the Doud genealogy and on Mrs. Doud's driver's license and car registration on exhibit in the museum, EL.

5. Ibid., 6–8, 10; "Doud Genealogy Chart," EL; "Ancestor Table #7, Mamie Eisenhower," in *24 Famous Swedish Americans and Their Ancestors* (Stockholm: Federation of Swedish Genealogical Society, 1996), 77, 79; Tom Branigar, archivist, EL, to author, Jan. 17, 2006.

6. Eisenhower, *Mrs. Ike,* 10–11, 17.

7. Ibid., 12, 14, 15; MDE to Douds, Nov. 15, 1930, box 1, family letters 1930 file, and MDE to Douds, Nov. 1934, box 2, family letters 1934 file, BE Papers, EL.

8. Eisenhower, *Mrs. Ike,* 12, 20; exhibit script, Rauch and Lang Electric Automobile, museum, EL.

9. MDE oral history, 118, EL; Eisenhower, *Mrs. Ike,* 20–21.

10. Maureen Honey, *Breaking the Ties That Bind: Popular Stories of the New Woman, 1915–1930* (Norman: University of Oklahoma Press, 1992), 4; John S. D. Eisenhower, *Strictly Personal* (Garden City, NY: Doubleday, 1974), 13–14. Other references to the New Woman and the Outdoor Girl can be found in Lois Rudnick, "The New Woman," in *1915, The Cultural Moment,* ed. Adele Heller and Lois Rudnick (New Brunswick, NJ: Rutgers University Press, 1991), and Rosalind Rosenberg, *Separate Spheres: Intellectual Roots of Modern Feminism* (New Haven, CT: Yale University Press, 1982).

11. Eisenhower, *Mrs. Ike,* 12; Dwight D. Eisenhower, *At Ease: Stories I Tell to Friends* (Garden City, NY: Doubleday, 1967), 184; MDE to Douds, Mar. 9, 1938,

box 2, family letters 1938 (1) file, and MDE to Douds, July 1935, box 2, family letters 1935 file (1), BE Papers, EL.

12. Eisenhower, *Mrs. Ike,* 34.

13. Ibid.; Eisenhower, *At Ease,* 112–113; MDE to Douds, Apr. 1940, box 3, family letters 1940 file (2), BE Papers, EL.

14. Eisenhower, *At Ease,* 112–113; Eisenhower, *Mrs. Ike,* 35.

15. Daniel D. Holt and James W. Leyerzapf, eds., *Eisenhower: The Prewar Diaries and Selected Papers, 1905–1941* (Baltimore: Johns Hopkins University Press, 1998), 7.

16. Beth L. Bailey, *From Front Porch to Back Seat: Courtship in Twentieth-Century America* (Baltimore: Johns Hopkins University Press, 1989), 13, 15–16; Eisenhower, *At Ease,* 113–117; Dorothy Brandon, *Mamie Doud Eisenhower: A Portrait of a First Lady* (New York: Scribner's, 1954), 57–58; Eisenhower, *Mrs. Ike,* 35, 36, 37; MDE oral history, 1, EL; Dennis Medina, museum curator, EL, interview with author, Aug. 17, 2006.

17. Eisenhower, *At Ease,* 117–118; MDE oral history, 117, EL.

18. Eisenhower, *Mrs. Ike,* 40; Eisenhower, *At Ease,* 121.

19. Eisenhower, *At Ease,* 74.

20. Ibid., 123; Eisenhower, *Mrs. Ike,* 42.

21. Eisenhower, *Mrs. Ike,* 42, 291; MDE oral history, 18–19, 47, EL; Martin M. Teasley, "Ike Was Her Career," *Prologue* 19 (Summer 1987): 114; Dennis Medina interview with author.

22. Eisenhower, *At Ease,* 123, 124; Brandon, *Mamie Doud Eisenhower,* 37; MDE oral history, 10, EL.

23. Eisenhower, *At Ease,* 125.

24. Eisenhower, *Mrs. Ike,* 15, 19; Carl Sferrazza Anthony, *America's First Families: An Inside View of 200 Years of Private Life in the White House* (New York: Touchstone, Simon and Schuster, 2000), 79; Eisenhower, *Strictly Personal,* 10–11.

25. Eisenhower, *Mrs. Ike,* 51–52; Holt and Leyerzapf, *Eisenhower: The Prewar Diaries,* 13, 16.

26. Eisenhower, *Mrs. Ike,* 55–56; Eisenhower, *At Ease,* 151; MDE oral history, 7, EL.

27. Eisenhower, *At Ease,* 174, 176.

28. MDE oral history, 14–15, EL.

29. Ibid., 39; MDE to Douds, Dec. 1933, box 2, family letters 1933 file (3), BE Papers, EL.

30. Eisenhower, *At Ease,* 180–182; Eisenhower, *Mrs. Ike,* 65; MDE to Douds, Oct. 1940, box 3 family letters 1940 file (4), and MDE to Douds, Sept. 24, 1943, box 4, family letters 1943 file (3), BE Papers, EL.

31. MDE oral history, 18–20, EL; Eisenhower, *At Ease,* 184; Brandon, *Mamie Doud Eisenhower,* 135.

32. Virginia Conner, *What Father Forbad* (Philadelphia: Dorrance, 1951), 120–121; Brandon, *Mamie Doud Eisenhower,* 136.

33. Brandon, *Mamie Doud Eisenhower,* 139; Eisenhower, *At Ease,* 194; MDE oral history, 21, EL.

34. Eisenhower, *Mrs. Ike,* 81–83.

35. MDE to Douds, Dec. 1922, box 1, family letters 1922 file, BE Papers, EL; MDE oral history, 21, EL; Brandon, *Mamie Doud Eisenhower,* 143–145; Conner, *What Father Forbad,* 120–121.

36. Holt and Leyerzapf, *Eisenhower: The Prewar Diaries,* xxiii–xxiv, 2, 59; MDE oral history, 9, 11, EL.

37. MDE to John Doud, June 10, 1929, box 1, family letters 1929 file (2), and MDE to Douds, Dec. 25, 1928, box 1 family letters 1928 file, BE Papers, EL; Eisenhower, *At Ease,* 206; Eisenhower, *Strictly Personal,* 2–3; MDE oral history, 10, EL; Holt and Leyerzapf, *Eisenhower: The Prewar Diaries,* 83.

38. Holt and Leyerzapf, *Eisenhower: The Prewar Diaries,* 84; MDE to Douds, Apr. 17, 1929, box 1, family letters 1929 file (1), BE Papers, EL.

39. Holt and Leyerzapf, *Eisenhower: The Prewar Diaries,* 92–93.

40. Ibid., 211, 213; MDE to Douds, 1932, box 1, family letters 1932 file (1), BE Papers, EL.

41. MDE to Douds, [July] 1932, box 1, family letters file (3), BE Papers, EL.

42. Eisenhower, *At Ease,* 155, 229–230; MDE oral history, 8–9, EL.

43. MDE to John Doud, June 10, 1929, box 1, family letters 1929 file (2), and MDE to John Doud, July 1932, box 1, family letters 1932 file (3), BE Papers, EL; MDE oral history, 36, EL; Holt and Leyerzapf, *Eisenhower: The Prewar Diaries,* 224, 251; Eisenhower, *Strictly Personal,* 8.

44. Eisenhower, *Mrs. Ike,* 113; John S. D. Eisenhower to author, June 21, 2006; White House invitation and admittance card, Jan. 21, 1932, box 1, family letters 1932 file (1), BE Papers, EL. For a representation of congressmen and cabinet members of Eisenhower's acquaintance, see Holt and Leyerzapf, *Eisenhower: The Prewar Diaries,* 168–169, 224–231.

45. Eisenhower, *Strictly Personal,* 10; Brandon, *Mamie Doud Eisenhower,* 42, 114; MDE to Douds, Oct. 1930 and Nov. 1930, box 1, family letters 1930 file, and

July 1932, fall 1932, box 1, family letters 1932 file (1 and 3), BE Papers, EL; Holt and Leyerzapf, *Eisenhower: The Prewar Diaries,* 145, 189, 548.

46. MDE to Douds, May 1935, box 2, family letters 1935 file (1), BE Papers, EL; Eisenhower, *At Ease,* 224; Brandon, *Mamie Doud Eisenhower,* 174, 178; "Mrs. D. D. Eisenhower's Medical History, 7/20/31–8/31/38," Mrs. D. D. Eisenhower medical records file, Sullivan Papers, EL; Holt and Leyerzapf, *Eisenhower: The Prewar Diaries,* 282.

47. Holt and Leyerzapf, *Eisenhower: The Prewar Diaries,* 11, 332–333, 549; Eisenhower, *Mrs. Ike,* 137–138, 145.

48. Eisenhower, *Mrs. Ike,* 145–146; MDE to Douds, Easter Sunday 1938, box 2, family letters 1938 file, BE Papers, EL.

49. Eisenhower, *Strictly Personal,* 9–11, 20; Holt and Leyerzapf, *Eisenhower: The Prewar Diaries,* 370, 432.

50. MDE oral history, 65, EL; MDE to Douds, May 7, 1937, and Aug. 19, 1937, box 2, family letters 1937 file (1), BE Papers, EL; Eisenhower, *Mrs. Ike,* 147, 153; Brandon, *Mamie Doud Eisenhower,* 197–198.

51. Daniel D. Holt, "An Unlikely Partnership and Service: Dwight Eisenhower, Mark Clark, and the Philippines," *Kansas History* 13 (Autumn 1990): 157; Eisenhower, *Mrs. Ike,* 154–155; Holt and Leyerzapf, *Eisenhower: The Prewar Diaries,* 400; "Mrs. D. D. Eisenhower's Medical History, 7/20/31–8/31/38," Mrs. D. D. Eisenhower medical records file, Sullivan Papers, EL; Carlo D'Este, *Eisenhower: A Soldier's Story* (New York: Holt, 2002), 245. The 1938 surgery has sometimes been confused with an earlier gallbladder surgery; later medical records stated that the latter surgery occurred in 1933, but medical records in the Sullivan Papers and a 1931 Eisenhower letter (Holt and Leyerzapf, *Eisenhower: The Prewar Diaries,* 189) point to 1931.

52. Brandon, *Mamie Doud Eisenhower,* 186; Holt, "An Unlikely Partnership," 158; MDE to Douds, Aug. 11, 1939, and Aug. 17, 1939, box 2, family letters 1939 file (5), BE Papers, EL.

53. Holt, "An Unlikely Partnership," 158, 160; Eisenhower, *Strictly Personal,* 27; MDE to Douds, Apr. 4, 1938, box 2, family letters 1938 file, BE Papers, EL; D'Este, *Eisenhower: A Soldier's Story,* 246.

54. MDE to Douds, Dec. 10, 1939, box 2, family letters 1939 file (6), BE Papers, EL; Holt, "An Unlikely Partnership," 160–161.

55. Holt and Leyerzapf, *Eisenhower: The Prewar Diaries,* 455; Brandon, *Mamie Doud Eisenhower,* 201; MDE to Douds, Dec. 15, 1939, box 2, family letters 1939 file (6), BE Papers, EL.

56. Holt and Leyerzapf, *Eisenhower: The Prewar Diaries,* 456, 460; MDE to Douds, Dec. 30, 1939, box 2, family letters 1939 file (6), BE Papers, EL; Eisenhower, *Mrs. Ike,* 158.

THE WAR YEARS LEAD TO THE WHITE HOUSE

1. Holt, "An Unlikely Partnership," 162; Holt and Leyerzapf, *Eisenhower: The Prewar Diaries,* 529–530.

2. MDE oral history, 98, EL; Holt and Leyerzapf, *Eisenhower: The Prewar Diaries,* 529–530, 549.

3. Holt, "An Unlikely Partnership," 162; Holt and Leyerzapf, *Eisenhower: The Prewar Diaries,* 489; MDE to Douds, Dec. 1941, box 3, family letters 1941 file (3), Jan. 1942, box 3, family letters 1942 file (1), BE Papers, EL.

4. Eisenhower, *Mrs. Ike,* 175; MDE to Douds, Jan. 1942, box 3, family letters 1942 file (1), BE Papers, EL. For itemized list of possessions, see Holt and Leyerzapf, *Eisenhower: The Prewar Diaries,* 524–529.

5. Eisenhower, *Mrs. Ike,* 175–176; MDE to Douds, Jan. 1942, Feb. 1942, box 3, family letters 1942 file (1), BE Papers, EL.

6. MDE to Barbara Ann Filey, Feb. 11, 1963, box 1, School Notes, Miscellaneous file, MDE Papers, 1963 Files Series, EL; MDE oral history, 1, EL.

7. MDE oral history, 94–95, EL; MDE to Douds, Apr. 1942, Sept. 1942, box 3, family letters files (2, 3), BE Papers, EL.

8. MDE oral history, 94–95, EL; Maurine Clark, *Captain's Bride, General's Lady: The Memoirs of Mrs. Mark Clark* (New York: McGraw-Hill, 1956), 111–113; MDE to Douds, Oct. 1940, box 3, family letters 1940 file (4), Sept. 24, 1943, and Oct. 30, 1943, box 4, family letters 1943 file (3), BE Papers, EL; D'Este, *Eisenhower: A Soldier's Story,* 313.

9. John S. D. Eisenhower, *Letters to Mamie: Dwight D. Eisenhower* (Garden City, NY: Doubleday, 1978), 19–20; Eisenhower, *Mrs. Ike,* 181; D'Este, *Eisenhower: A Soldier's Story,* 310–312; MDE to Douds, Sept. 1942, box 3, family letters 1942 file (3), BE Papers, EL; MDE oral history, 87–88, EL.

10. MDE to Douds, July 1942, box 3, family letters 1942 file (3), Sept. 24, 1943, box 4, family letters 1943 file (3), and May 14, 1945, box 4, family letters 1945 file, BE Papers, EL.

11. David Brinkley, *Washington Goes to War* (New York: Ballantine Books, 1988), 105–106; Eisenhower, *Mrs. Ike,* 184.

12. Brandon, *Mamie Doud Eisenhower,* 229; MDE to Douds, July 1942, box 3, family letters 1942 file (3), DDE to Douds, June 17, 1943, and Mar. 15, 1943, box 3, family letters 1943 file (1, 2), MDE to Douds, Dec. 1943, box 4,

family letters 1943 file (4), Apr. 1945, box 4, family letters 1945 file, BE Papers, EL.

13. Elizabeth Henney, "Presenting: Mrs. Eisenhower," *Washington Post,* Aug. 2, 1942, clipping, box 34, Photographs, Newspaper Clippings file, MDE Papers, White House Series, EL.

14. Ibid.

15. Eisenhower, *Mrs. Ike,* 199, 204.

16. Brinkley, *Washington Goes to War,* 141–143, 151; MDE to Douds, June 17, 1943, box 3, family letters 1943 file (2), Sept. 24, 1943, box 4, family letters 1943 file (3), BE Papers, EL; MDE oral history, 95, EL.

17. MDE oral history, 89, EL; MDE to Douds, Jan. 21, 1943, Feb. 1943, May 30, 1943, box 3, family letters 1943 file (1, 2), Sept. 5, 1943, Sept. 24, 1943, Dec. 18, 1943, box 4, family letters file (3, 4), and invitation with visitor's pass, Nov. 18, 1943, box 4, family letters 1943 file (4), BE Papers, EL; Eisenhower, *Mrs. Ike,* 213; MDE interview with Barbara Walters, NBC, Mar. 26, 1970, video, EL; Teasley, "Ike Was Her Career," 112.

18. Eisenhower, *Mrs. Ike,* 195; MDE to Douds, Jan. 28, 1942, box 3, family letters 1943 file (1), BE Papers, EL.

19. D'Este, *Eisenhower: A Soldier's Story,* 313; Steve Neal, *The Eisenhowers: Reluctant Dynasty* (Garden City, NY: Doubleday, 1978), 463; MDE to Douds, Apr. 1945, box 4, family letters 1945 file, BE Papers, EL.

20. D'Este, *Eisenhower: A Soldier's Story,* 312–313; MDE oral history, 92–93, EL; Lightfoot Solomon Michaux to MDE, Feb. 10, 1958, and Mary Jane McCaffree to Elder Michaux, Feb. 11, 1958, box 3, Personal—MDE file (6), MDE Papers, White House Series, EL.

21. D'Este, *Eisenhower: A Soldier's Story,* 313; MDE oral history, 90, EL.

22. "General 'Ike' Eisenhower," *Life,* Nov. 9, 1942, 122–123; Collection Description, Wyden Papers, EL; D'Este, *Eisenhower: A Soldier's Story,* 387, 388, 389, 419–420.

23. D'Este, *Eisenhower: A Soldier's Story,* 387, 388; Eisenhower, *Letters to Mamie,* 97; DDE to Douds, Jan. 20, 1943, box 3, family letters 1943 file (1), and MDE to Douds, Aug. 20, 1943, box 4, family letters 1943 file (3), BE Papers, EL. Mamie mistakenly identified Bourke-White as Margaret Burke Smith.

24. D'Este, *Eisenhower: A Soldier's Story,* 419, 543; Kay Summersby, *Eisenhower Was My Boss* (New York: Prentice-Hall, 1948), 155, 157, 159, 161; "Kay's War," *Time,* Sept. 27, 1948, 26.

25. Robert H. Ferrell, ed., *The Eisenhower Diaries* (New York: Norton, 1981), 145; "Kay's War," 26; MDE to Douds, Sept. 27, 1948, box 4, family letters 1948 file,

BE Papers, EL. For Butcher and McKeogh publications, see Harry Butcher, *My Three Years with Eisenhower* (New York: Simon and Schuster, 1946), and Michael J. McKeogh and Richard Lockeridge, *Sgt. Mickey and General Ike* (New York: Putnam's, 1946).

26. D'Este, *Eisenhower: A Soldier's Story,* 419–420; Eisenhower, *Letters to Mamie,* 11–12; Stephen E. Ambrose, *Eisenhower: Soldier, General of the Army, President-Elect, 1890–1952,* vol. 1 (New York: Simon and Schuster, 1983), 417–418; Kay Summersby Morgan, *Past Forgetting: My Love Affair with Dwight D. Eisenhower* (New York: Simon and Schuster, 1975). The ghostwriter was Barbara Wyden; see Wyden Papers, EL.

27. Eisenhower, *Letters to Mamie,* 35; McKeogh and Lockeridge, *Sgt. Mickey and General Ike,* 54; Gordon Moore to MDE, Nov. 23, 1943, box 4, family letters 1943 file (4), DDE to Douds, Jan. 20, 1943, and MDE to Douds, Feb. 9, 1943, box 3, family letters 1943 file (1), BE Papers, EL; MDE oral history, 312, EL.

28. Brandon, *Mamie Doud Eisenhower,* 222–223; MDE oral history, 102, EL; Eisenhower, *Letters to Mamie,* 161, 164, 165.

29. Eisenhower, *Mrs. Ike,* 221; D'Este, *Eisenhower: A Soldier's Story,* 540.

30. Eisenhower, *Letters to Mamie,* 220–222.

31. Ibid., 255; MDE to Douds, May 14, 1945, box 4, family letters 1945 file, BE Papers, EL.

32. McKeogh and Lockeridge, *Sgt. Mickey and General Ike,* 179, 181; MDE to Douds, May 14, 1945, box 4, family letters 1945 file, BE Papers, EL.

33. Eisenhower, *At Ease,* 316; Brandon, *Mamie Doud Eisenhower,* 249; Eisenhower, *Strictly Personal,* 124–125.

34. MDE to Douds, May 14, 1945, box 4, family letters 1945 file, BE Papers, EL; Eisenhower, *Mrs. Ike,* 254; Conner, *What Father Forbad,* 121–122.

35. Eisenhower, *At Ease,* 334, 336; Ambrose, *Eisenhower: Soldier, General of the Army, President-Elect,* 469–470; "A Friend," to MDE, May 3 and May 7, 1948, box 1, Appeals and Crank Letters file (1), MDE Papers, Columbia Series, EL.

36. Eisenhower, *At Ease,* 339; Eisenhower, *Mrs. Ike,* 252; "Mr. President: As the Head of a Great University," *Life,* Apr. 17, 1950, 144–150.

37. Travis Beal Jacobs, *Eisenhower at Columbia* (New Brunswick, NJ: Transaction, 2001), 196–197, 199; MDE to Douds, Mar. 1949, and Al Gruenther to MDE, July 7, 1949, box 4, family letters 1949 file, BE Papers, EL.

38. Eisenhower, *At Ease,* 368; Brandon, *Mamie Doud Eisenhower,* 268; Eisenhower, *Mrs. Ike,* 258.

39. Ambrose, *Eisenhower: Soldier, General of the Army, President-Elect,* 514–520; Eisenhower, *At Ease,* 377; A. Marjorie Day to MDE, Oct. 11, 1951, and

D. W. Dailey to MDE, Mar. 21, 1952, box 1, D file, MDE Papers, SHAPE Series, EL; MDE to Elivera Doud, Dec. 27, 1951, box 4, family letters 1951, BE Papers, EL.

40. Collection Description, Cochran Papers, EL.

41. Brandon, *Mamie Doud Eisenhower,* 273–274; Eisenhower, *At Ease,* 378; MDE to Jacqueline Cochran, May 20, 1952, Eisenhower file (1), General Files Series, Cochran Papers, EL.

42. William Anderson to Jacqueline Cochran, Jan. 1954, box 259, Eisenhower file (1), General Files Series, Cochran Papers, EL; Ambrose, *Eisenhower: Soldier, General of the Army, President-Elect,* 524, 530; Jon Roe, "Ike and TV: The Perfect Political Pair," *Wichita (KS) Eagle,* Apr. 10, 1990, 1A; Craig Allen, *Eisenhower and the Mass Media: Peace, Prosperity, and Prime-Time TV* (Chapel Hill: University of North Carolina Press, 1993), 31–32; Bernard Benjamin Yamron, "From Whistle Stops to Polispots: Political Advertising and Presidential Politics in the United States, 1948–1980" (Ph.D. diss., Brown University, 1995), 29–31; Nina Davis (Mrs. T. J.) to MDE, Sept. 29, 1952, box 10, Davi file, MDE Papers, White House Series, EL.

43. Ambrose, *Eisenhower: Soldier, General of the Army, President-Elect,* 532–534; Brandon, *Mamie Doud Eisenhower,* 79–82; MDE oral history, 150, EL.

44. Lucy Freeman, "Wife Says General Excels as Painter," *New York Times,* July 13, 1952, 50; "Mamie Emerges as Poised Campaigner," *Life,* July 21, 1952, 22–23.

45. Ambrose, *Eisenhower: Soldier, General of the Army, President-Elect,* 538–540; Dwight D. Eisenhower, *The White House Years: Mandate for Change, 1953–1956* (Garden City, NY: Doubleday, 1963), 44; Brandon, *Mamie Doud Eisenhower,* 300; Abbott Washburn, panel discussion, Nov. 16, 1996, MDE Centennial, EL; Ruth Butcher to MDE, July 11, 1952, box 5, Mrs. Ruth Butcher file, and MDE to Marjorie Davis, July 25, 1952, box 10, Mrs. Joseph Davis file, MDE Papers, White House Series, EL.

46. Gabriel Hauge Biography, typescript, pp. 1, 4, 5, box 1, Chapter 8 file, Bookman Papers, EL; Robert Wallace, "They Like Mamie Too," *Life,* Oct. 13, 1952, 149–150; Brandon, *Mamie Doud Eisenhower,* 274; "Mamie" video, Presidential Gallery, museum, EL.

47. Ambrose, *Eisenhower: Soldier, General of the Army, President-Elect,* 551; Gabriel Hauge Biography, p. 5, box 1, Chapter 8 file, Bookman Papers, EL; Eisenhower, *Mrs. Ike,* 273.

48. Brandon, *Mamie Doud Eisenhower,* 296, 300; Julie Nixon Eisenhower, *Special People* (New York: Simon and Schuster, 1977), 188; Steve Benedict to author, Nov. 1, 2006; MDE to Marjorie Davis, Oct. 11, 1952, box 10, Mrs. Joseph C.

Davis file, and MDE to Helen Davis, Oct. 11, 1952, box 10, Davi file, MDE Papers, White House Series, EL.

49. Steve Benedict to author, Nov. 1, 2006; MDE oral history, 150, EL.

50. Eisenhower, *Strictly Personal*, 170; Steve Neal, ed., *Eleanor and Harry: The Correspondence of Eleanor Roosevelt and Harry S. Truman* (New York: Scribner, 2002), 223; Joseph P. Lash, *A World of Love: Eleanor Roosevelt and Her Friends, 1942–1962* (Garden City, NY: Doubleday, 1984), 385; Susan Eisenhower, panel discussion, MDE Centennial, EL; Lester David and Irene David, *Ike and Mamie: The Story of the General and His Lady* (New York: Putnam's, 1981), 187; MDE interview with Barbara Walters, Nov. 1, 1979, ABC *20/20*, video, EL.

51. Ambrose, *Eisenhower: Soldier, General of the Army, President-Elect*, 554, 557.

52. "Mamie Emerges as Poised Campaigner," *Life*, July 21, 1952, 23; Steve Benedict to author, Nov. 1, 2006; Julie Nixon Eisenhower, *Pat Nixon: The Untold Story* (New York: Simon and Schuster, 1986), 123, 125–126.

53. Brandon, *Mamie Doud Eisenhower*, 301; MDE oral history, 152, EL; Margaret Truman, *First Ladies* (New York: Random House, 1995), 214; J. B. West, *Upstairs at the White House: My Life with the First Ladies* (New York: Coward, McCann and Geoghegan, 1973), 89.

54. Anthony, *America's First Families*, 28; "Inauguration," *Life*, Feb. 2, 1953, 19.

BEING FIRST LADY IN THE 1950S

1. Ruth Butcher to MDE, 1953, box 5, Mrs. Ruth Butcher file, MDE Papers, White House Series, EL; MDE to Al Gruenther, Jan. 26, 1953, box 3, MDE 1953 file (2), E. Corres. Series, Gruenther Papers, EL.

2. "The General's Lady," *Time*, June 2, 1952 21–22; West, *Upstairs at the White House*, 132; Robert Wallace, "They Like Mamie Too," *Life*, Oct. 13, 1952, 149–150; "Ike and Mamie: What They'll Be Like . . . ," *U.S News & World Report*, Nov. 14, 1952, 54–55.

3. MDE interview with Barbara Walters, Mar. 26, 1970, NBC, video, EL; Eisenhower, *Mrs. Ike*, 160; Brandon, *Mamie Doud Eisenhower*, 251; MDE to Bella Hall, Apr. 29, 1953, box 17, Hal file, MDE Papers, White House Series, EL.

4. "Mrs. Eisenhower Receives 300 Republicans at Reception in Busy White House Day," *New York Times*, Jan. 22, 1953, clipping, box 1, Scrapbook 1, MDE Scrapbooks, White House Social Office, EL; MDE to Perle Mesta, Dec. 8, 1952, box 29, Mrs. Perle Mesta file, and "Mrs. Eisenhower's First Press and Radio Conference," Mar. 11, 1953, transcript, box 35, Press (1952–1953) file (1), MDE Papers, White House Series, EL; Bess Furman, "Keeping House at the White

House," *New York Times Magazine,* Dec. 28, 1952, sec. 6, pp. 7, 23; West, *Upstairs at the White House,* 136.

5. Marjorie Davis to MDE, Feb. 6, 1954, box 10, Mrs. Joseph C. Davis file, MDE Papers, White House Series, EL; Susan Eisenhower and Mary Jane McCaffree Monroe, panel discussion, MDE Centennial, EL.

6. Teasley, "Ike Was Her Career," 112; Eisenhower, *Mrs. Ike,* 256–257, 287; Eisenhower, *At Ease,* 360. The Elisabeth C. Draper Papers, 1948–1980, EL, include 1955 materials related to costs and correspondence.

7. "Next President: A Rich Man," *U.S. News & World Reports,* Oct. 10, 1952, 15–16; Steven Mintz and Susan Kellogg, *Domestic Revolutions: A Social History of American Family Life* (New York: Free Press, 1988), 183; Clifford E. Clark Jr., "Ranch-House Suburbia: Ideals and Realities," in *Recasting America: Culture and Politics in the Age of Cold War,* ed. Lary May (Chicago: University of Chicago Press, 1989), 183.

8. Barbara Eisenhower Foltz, phone interview with author, Nov. 13, 2006; "Is Ike to Be Underpaid?" *U.S. News & World Report,* Jan. 16, 1953, 29, 43–44.

9. Exhibit script, Mamie Gallery, museum, EL; West, *Upstairs at the White House,* 145–156; Brandon, *Mamie Doud Eisenhower,* 247, 268; Rex Scouten, panel discussion, MDE Centennial, EL; Dennis Medina interview with author.

10. "Medical Records of Mrs. Dwight D. Eisenhower," and Dr. G. P. Robb and Dr. Howard Snyder, "Consultation Request and Report," Jan. 4, 1946, and Dr. Thomas W. Mattingly, "Doctor's Progress Notes," Nov. 5, 1951, box 4, Mamie Doud Eisenhower file, Mattingly Papers, EL; C. L. Sulzberger, *A Long Row of Candles: Memoirs and Diaries (1934–1954)* (New York: Macmillan, 1969), 919.

11. West, *Upstairs at the White House,* 145; Rex Scouten, panel discussion, MDE Centennial, EL; "Mrs. Eisenhower's First Press and Radio Conference," and "Appointments for Week Beginning February 22," box 35, Press (1952–1953) file (1), MDE Papers, White House Series, EL; Truman, *First Ladies,* 85; Barbara A. Perry, *Jacqueline Kennedy: First Lady of the New Frontier* (Lawrence: University Press of Kansas, 2004), 74.

12. West, *Upstairs at the White House,* 131, 155.

13. Eisenhower, *The White House Years: Mandate for Change,* 265; Teasley, "Ike Was Her Career," 111; West, *Upstairs at the White House,* 167–168; Betty Boyd Caroli, *First Ladies,* 2nd ed. (Garden City, NY: Doubleday Direct, 1997), 249; Josephine Ripley, "'A Part of History': An Intimate Message from Washington," *Christian Science Monitor,* ca. 1961, clipping, box 3, MDE 1961–1962 file, E. Corres. Series, Gruenther Papers, EL.

14. West, *Upstairs at the White House,* 130; Robert J. Donovan, *Confidential Secretary: Ann Whitman's 20 Years with Eisenhower and Rockefeller* (New York: Dutton, 1988), 14, 15; Collection Description, box 1, Correspondence—E file, Whitman Papers, EL; Eisenhower, *Mrs. Ike,* 277.

15. Donovan, *Confidential Secretary,* 132; West, *Upstairs at the White House,* 130, 131, 132, 155; Rex Scouten, panel discussion, MDE Centennial, EL; "Baby spoons and cups ordered from Mr. Stieff," box 2, Babies file, MDE Papers, White House Series, EL.

16. Teasley, "Ike Was Her Career," 114; West, *Upstairs at the White House,* 133; Rex Scouten, panel discussion, MDE Centennial, video, EL; MDE oral history, 11, EL; Eisenhower, *Mrs. Ike,* 277; Walter Trohan, *Political Animals: Memories of a Sentimental Cynic* (Garden City, NY: Doubleday, 1975), 291, 368; Pat Nixon to Helene Drown, Feb. 3, 1953, Helene Drown Collection, Nixon Library.

17. Eisenhower, *Mrs. Ike,* 277; MDE interview with Vivian Cadden, typescript, p. 4, box 2, Ca file (1), MDE Papers, 1966 Files Series, EL.

18. John L. Helgerson, *Getting to Know the President: CIA Briefings of Presidential Candidates, 1952–1992* (Washington, DC: Center for the Study of Intelligence, Central Intelligence Agency, ca. 1994), 33, 34–35; Neal, *The Eisenhowers,* 401; Perry, *Jacqueline Kennedy,* 11.

19. Joanne Meyerowitz, "Beyond the Feminine Mystique: A Reassessment of Postwar Mass Culture, 1946–1958," in *Not June Cleaver: Women and Gender in Postwar America, 1945–1960,* ed. Joanne Meyerowitz (Philadelphia: Temple University Press, 1994), 230–231; Elaine Tyler May, *Homeward Bound: American Families in the Cold War Era,* rev. ed. (New York: Basic Books, 1999), 187; William H. Chafe, *The Paradox of Change: American Women in the 20th Century* (New York: Oxford University Press, 1991), 176, 196; Clark, "Ranch-House Suburbia," 172–173.

20. Robert W. Smuts, *Women and Work in America* (New York: Columbia University Press, 1959), 60; National Manpower Council, *Womanpower: A Statement by the National Manpower Council* (New York: Columbia University Press, 1957), 56, 315; "The Effects on Children and Youth of the Employment of the Mother Outside the Home," information worksheet, 1958, Workgroups 29–30, box 120, folder 3, Central Files, White House Conference on Children and Youth: Records, 1930–1970, EL; "Mrs. Ridgway to Center Interest on Art," *Times-Herald,* July 5, 1953, box 9, Clippings—Friends of MDE file, MDE Papers, White House Series, EL.

21. May, *Homeward Bound,* 90; Oveta Culp Hobby, exhibit script, Presidential Gallery, museum, EL.

22. Gil Troy, *Mr. & Mrs. President: From the Trumans to the Clintons,* 2nd ed. rev. (Lawrence: University Press of Kansas, 2000), 127; Collection Description, Mary Pillsbury Lord Papers, 1941–1972, EL; DDE to Jacqueline Cochran Odum, Nov. 7, 1956, box 259, Eisenhower file (2), General Files Series, Cochran Papers, EL; Frances DeWolf, "Home, Family—'They Are My Life,'" *Palm Desert (CA) Daily Enterprise,* Apr. 26, 1963, box 1, News Clippings file (1), MDE Papers, 1963 Files Series, EL.

23. Mary Jane McCaffree Monroe, panel discussion, MDE Centennial, EL; Caroli, *First Ladies,* 229; "Mrs. Eisenhower's First Press and Radio Conference," MDE Papers, White House Series, EL; Inez Robb, "Mamie Is Just What Country Ordered," clipping, box 35, Press (1952–1953) file (1), MDE Papers, White House Series, EL.

24. Robb, "Mamie Is Just What Country Ordered," clipping, box 35, Press (1952–1953) file (1), MDE Papers, White House Series, EL.

25. Teasley, "Ike Was Her Career," 112–113; Murray Snyder to Mary Jane McCaffree, Jan. 31, 1955, box 35, Press (1955–1956) file, and Ruth Boyer Scott (*Progressive Farmer*) to Mary Jane McCaffree, June 27, 1953, and questionnaire, box 35, Press (1952–1953) file (1), and Jo Anne Morris to MDE, Dec. 7, 1952, MDE to Jo Anne Morris, Dec. 16, 1952, box 35, Requests file (1), and MDE to Ben Hibbs (*Saturday Evening Post*), Feb. 9, 1954, box 35, Press (1954) file (1), MDE Papers, White House Series, EL.

26. Max Rabb to Mary Jane McCaffree, Oct. 19, 1953, box 35, Press (1952–1953) file (2), MDE Papers, White House Series, and "Press Women Invited in Working Capacity Only," May 8, 1958, clipping, box 5, Scrapbook 5, MDE Scrap Book, White House Social Office, EL; Ripley, "'A Part of History': An Intimate Message from Washington," clipping, box 3, MDE 1961–1962 file, E. Corres. Series, Gruenther Papers, EL; Lonnelle Aikman, "Inside the White House," *National Geographic,* Jan. 1961, 19.

27. Lewis L. Gould, "Modern First Ladies: An Institutional Perspective," *Prologue* 19 (Summer 1987): 76; *White House Staff Book, 1953–61,* EL.

28. Teasley, "Ike Was Her Career," 112; *Publisher's Weekly,* Feb. 14, 1953, James Hagerty to Mary Jane McCaffree, Feb. 24, 1953, box 35, Press (1952–1953) file (1), and Drew Pearson, "The White House Soothsayer," *Washington Post,* Aug. 22, 1953, clipping, and James Hagerty to Drew Pearson, Aug. 26, 1953, box 35, Press (1952–1953) file (2), MDE Papers, White House Series, EL.

29. Holt and Leyerzapf, *Eisenhower: The Prewar Diaries,* 531; Oliver Pilat, *Drew Pearson: An Unauthorized Biography* (New York: Harper's Magazine Press, 1973), 222, 227; Tyler Abell, ed., *Drew Pearson Diaries, 1949–1959* (New York:

Holt, Rinehart and Winston, 1974), 435; "Mamie's High-Class Hideaway," *Life*, Mar. 10, 1958, 54; MDE to Elizabeth Arden Graham, Feb. 16, 1960, box 2, Elizabeth Arden file, MDE papers, White House Series, EL.

30. West, *Upstairs at the White House*, 166; W. Dale Nelson, *The President Is at Camp David* (Syracuse, NY: Syracuse University Press, 1995), 36–37; Abell, *Drew Pearson Diaries*, 454; MDE interview with Barbara Walters, Mar. 26, 1970, NBC, video, EL.

31. Brigadier General Arthur S. Nevins, *Gettysburg's Five-Star Farmer* (New York: Carlton Press, 1977), 87, 113; DDE to Jackie (Cochran) and Floyd Odum, Nov. 11, 1956, box 259, Eisenhower file (2), General Files Series, Cochran Papers, EL; Mary Jane McCaffree to Mrs. Stanley E. Prime, Aug. 24, 1954, box 36, Pri–Pru file, MDE Papers, White House Series, EL; Carl Sferrazza Anthony, *First Ladies: The Saga of the Presidents' Wives and Their Power, 1789–1961* (New York: Quill/William Morrow, 1990), 585; "Mamie & the Fur Trade," *Life*, Nov. 11, 1957, 26.

32. Barbara Eisenhower Foltz, interview with author; Mrs. John Eisenhower, "How to Be a Daughter-in-Law," *This Week: The National Sunday Magazine*, Feb. 15, 1953, clipping, box 35, Press Requests file (1), and MDE to Louise Caffey, box 5, Gen. & Mrs. Benjamin Caffey file, MDE Papers, White House Series, EL; Jack Harrison Pollack, "How Ike Rates as a Father," *This Week: The National Sunday Magazine*, June 16, 1957, 8–10; Elaine Tyler May, "Cold War—Warm Hearth," in *The Eisenhower Presidency and the 1950s*, ed. Michael S. Mayer (New York: Houghton Mifflin, 1998), 223; Barbara Eisenhower to James Hagerty, July 21, 1953, and James C. Hagerty to Alice Bambrick, Aug. 26, 1953, box 35, Press (1952–1953) file (2), MDE Papers, White House Series, EL.

33. Matilda Taylor to Mrs. John Eisenhower, Dec. 22, 1952, box 35, Press Requests file (1), MDE Papers, 1963 Files Series, EL.

34. "Meet Baby Ike," *Parents*, Nov. 1948, 24–25; "'First Boy' of the Land," *Chicago Tribune Magazine*, Oct. 2, 1955, clipping, box 1, News Clippings file (1), MDE Papers, 1963 Files Series, EL; Anthony, *First Families*, 114; Eisenhower, *Strictly Personal*, 172.

35. Brandon, *Mamie Doud Eisenhower*, 291; Caroli, *First Ladies*, 248; Eisenhower, *Mrs. Ike*, 282; MDE interview with Vivian Cadden, typescript, p. 2, box 2, Ca file (1), MDE Papers, 1966 Files Series, EL; Molly Parnis quotation, exhibit script, Mamie Gallery, museum, EL.

36. MDE to Douds, June 17, 1929, box 1, family letters 1929 file (2), and MDE to Douds, Sept. 24, 1930, box 1, family letters 1930 file, BE Papers, EL; Eisenhower, *Mrs. Ike*, 260, 286, 294.

37. "Taste in Garb Shown by Next First Lady," *New York Times,* Nov. 22, 1952, 20; Alice Hughes to MDE, Dec. 8, 1952, box 35, Press Requests file (2), MDE Papers, White House Series, EL.

38. "Taste in Garb Shown by Next First Lady," 20; Karal Ann Marling, *As Seen on TV: The Visual Culture of Everyday Life in the 1950s* (Cambridge, MA: Harvard University Press, 1994), 21.

39. "Mrs. Eisenhower Picks Wardrobe for Inaugural," *New York Herald Tribune,* Jan. 12, 1953, clipping, and press release, Jan. 13, 1953, box 35, Press Requests file (1), MDE Papers, White House Series, EL; Dennis Medina interview with author; Ripley, "'A Part of History': An Intimate Message from Washington," clipping, box 3, MDE 1961–1962 file, E. Corres. Series, Gruenther Papers, EL.

40. Anthony, *America's First Families,* 336; John B. Roberts II, *Rating the First Ladies: The Women Who Influenced the Presidency* (New York: Kensington, 2003), 270; Dennis Medina interview with author; Brian S. Alexander, *Atomic Kitchen: Gadgets and Inventions for Yesterday's Cook* (Portland, OR: Collectors Press, 2004), 16, 31, 92, 99, 106, 114; Eisenhower, *Pat Nixon,* 207–208.

41. MDE to Charlotte Duruz, Apr. 22, 1952, box 1, D file, MDE Papers, SHAPE Series, EL; Dennis Medina interview with author; Molly Parnis, Nettie Rosenstein, Irene, and Arnold Scaasi, exhibit scripts, museum, EL; "Scaasi Creates Gala Wardrobe for Mrs. Eisenhower," press release, Sept. 1959, box 33, Personal—MDE file (8), and "Mrs. Eisenhower's Easter Outfit," press release, Apr. 4, 1953, box 35, Press (1952–1953) file, and "Easter 1956," press release, 1956, box 35, Press (1955–1956) file, and Mollie Parnis Livingston to Mary Jane McCaffree, Apr. 14, 1955, box 32, Mollie Parnis (Livingston) file, and "First Lady's Inaugural Gown," press release, Jan. 18, 1957, box 24, Inauguration Dress 1957 file, MDE Papers, White House Series, EL.

42. Mary Jane McCaffree to MDE, 1959, box 33, Personal—MDE file (8), and MDE to Mollie Parnis, Oct. 26, 1956, box 32, Mollie Parnis (Livingston) file, MDE Papers, White House Series, EL; Dennis Medina interview with author; "Mrs. Eisenhower on List of Best-Dressed Women," *New York Times,* Dec. 17, 1952, 38; "The General's Lady," *Time,* June 2, 1952, 21.

43. Marling, *As Seen on TV,* 25–26; Helen Thomas to Mary Jane McCaffree, Sept. 2, 1953, and Mary Jane McCaffree memo, Sept. 1953, box 35, Press (1952–1953) file, and MDE to Bella Hall, Aug. 17, 1956, box 17, Hal file, MDE Papers, White House Series, EL.

44. "Ike" charm bracelet, exhibit, Mamie Gallery, museum, EL; "It Can Happen Even to the President's Wife," *New York Times,* Apr. 1, 1955, 29.

45. Mary Jane McCaffree memo, Sept. 1953, box 35, Press (1952–1953) file, and "Message from Mrs. Eisenhower to Editors Attending Press Week," Jan. 5, 1952, box 35, Press Requests file (1), MDE Papers, White House Series, EL; MDE to Douds, Mar. 12, 1931, box 1, family letters 1932 file (2), BE Papers, EL; Marling, *As Seen on TV,* 23–24.

46. Brandon, *Mamie Doud Eisenhower,* 136–137; Elizabeth Arden to MDE, Feb. 20, 1953, and copy of diagram/sketches, box 2, Elizabeth Arden file, and Chloris A. Maynard, *Life,* to MDE, Nov. 10, 1953, box 35, Press (1952–1952) file (2), MDE Papers, White House Series, EL; Elizabeth Arden diagram, exhibit, Mamie Gallery, museum, EL; Eisenhower, *Mrs. Ike,* 282.

47. Robb, "Mamie Is Just What Country Ordered," clipping, box 35, Press (1952–1953) file (1), MDE Papers, White House Series, EL.

ENTERTAINING AT HOME

1. Richard R. Cain, *Images of America: Eleanor Roosevelt's Valkill* (Charleston, SC: Arcadia, 2002), 28, 43; Brinkley, *Washington Goes to War,* 147; Robert Wallace, "They Like Mamie, Too," *Life,* Oct. 13, 1952, 158; "Ike and Mamie: What They'll Be Like," *U.S. News & World Report,* Nov. 14, 1952, 54; West, *Upstairs at the White House,* 364; Brandon, *Mamie Doud Eisenhower,* 251.

2. West, *Upstairs at the White House,* 364; "President and Wife Hosts to Diplomats," *Washington Evening Star,* Nov. 11, 1953, clipping, box 2, Scrapbook 2, White House Social Office, MDE Scrapbooks, EL; MDE to Grace Gruenther, Aug. 26, 1953, box 3, MDE 1953 file (1), E. Corres. Series, Gruenther Papers, EL; Bess Furman, "Mrs. Eisenhower Retains Role of 'Good Soldier' for General," *New York Times,* Mar. 1, 1956, 15.

3. Brandon, *Mamie Doud Eisenhower,* 148; MDE to Douds, Nov. 1933, box 1, family letters 1933 file (3), and MDE to Douds, Nov. 1940, box 3, family letters 1940 file (4), BE Papers, EL.

4. MDE interview with Barbara Walters, Mar. 26, 1970, NBC, video, EL; Teasley, "Ike Was Her Career," 108; Brandon, *Mamie Doud Eisenhower,* 271; MDE to Elivera Doud, Mar. 2, 1952, box 4, family letters 1952 file, BE Papers, EL; Nancy Beck Young, *Lou Henry Hoover: Activist First Lady* (Lawrence: University Press of Kansas, 2004), 54–56.

5. MDE to Bella Hall, May 29, 1958, box 17, Hal file, MDE Papers, White House Series, EL; MDE oral history, 171, EL; Eisenhower, *Mrs. Ike,* 281; Dwight D. Eisenhower, *The White House Years: Waging Peace, 1956–1961* (Garden City, NY: Doubleday, 1965), 171, 404.

6. Exhibit script, Mamie Gallery, museum, EL; Martin M. Teasley, "Mamie (Geneva Doud) Eisenhower," in *American First Ladies: Their Lives and Their Legacy,* ed. Lewis L. Gould (New York: Routledge, 2001), 471.

7. Exhibit script, Mamie Gallery, museum, EL; MDE oral history, 163, EL; Mary Jane McCaffree and Pauline Innis, *Protocol: The Complete Handbook of Diplomatic, Official and Social Usage* (1977; reprint, Washington, DC: Devon, 1985), xvi; Furman, "Mrs. Eisenhower Retains Role of 'Good Soldier' for General," 15.

8. "A Rare Picture Visit: The First Lady at Home," *Life,* Oct. 20, 1958, 60–65; Eisenhower, *Mandate for Change,* 264; Elise K. Kirk, *Music at the White House: A History of the American Spirit* (Urbana: University of Illinois Press, 1986), 268, 271, 274.

9. David and David, *Ike and Mamie;* Lewis L. Gould, *Lady Bird Johnson: Our Environmental First Lady* (Lawrence: University Press of Kansas, 1999), 30; Eisenhower, *Mrs. Ike,* 298; "Dr. Snyder's Patient," *Time,* Aug. 19, 1957, 9.

10. West, *Upstairs at the White House,* 135; Aikman, "Inside the White House," 43; Ripley, "'A Part of History,'" clipping, box 3, MDE 1961–1962 file, E. Corres. Series, Gruenther Papers, EL.

11. McCaffree and Innis, *Protocol,* xvi, xvii, 1; memos, Sept. 19, Sept. 22, 1955, box 4, Background Information re Foreign Visitors file, and Notes on Protocol, box 4, Rules and Protocol file, McCaffree Papers, EL; Anthony, *First Ladies,* 580.

12. Donovan, *Confidential Secretary,* 122–123.

13. West, *Upstairs at the White House,* 185; Eisenhower, *Waging Peace,* 439; "Russia's First Lady in Good American Hands," *Life,* Sept. 28, 1959, 35.

14. Stephen E. Ambrose, *Eisenhower: The President* (New York: Simon and Schuster, 1984), 543–544; Barbara Eisenhower Foltz interview with author; Eisenhower, *Waging Peace,* 444.

15. Eisenhower, *Mandate for Change,* 507.

16. Ibid., 241, 510; "President Begins Talks in Ottawa," *New York Times,* July 9, 1958, 1, 3; Eleanor Roosevelt, *This I Remember* (New York: Harper and Brothers, 1949), 287; Margaret Truman, *Harry S. Truman* (New York: Morrow, 1973), 374–375; Lynn Bassanese, Roosevelt Presidential Library, to EL, Sept. 7, 2006; Michael Devine, Truman Presidential Library, to EL, Sept. 7, 2006.

17. Eisenhower, *Mandate for Change,* 511, 512, 517; "Persons Whom Mrs. Eisenhower Met, Trip to Geneva, Switzerland, July 16–25, 1955," box 14, Geneva Summit Meeting file, MDE Papers, White House Series, EL; "Eisenhower Party Begins to Break Geneva Camp," *New York Times,* July 23, 1955, 3; MDE to Kitty Smith, July 26, 1955, box 39, Gen. and Mrs. Howard Smith file, MDE Papers, White House Series, EL.

18. "Tea at the White House, June 4, 1953," box 10, Wives of Representatives—Tea file (1, 2), White House Social Office, Tolley, EL; "guest list, May 5, 1960," box 6, Scrapbook 6, White House Social Office, MDE Scrapbooks, EL; MDE to Grace Gruenther, Nov. 16, 1953, box 3, MDE 1952 file (1), E. Corres. Series, Gruenther Papers, and MDE to Bella Hall, box 17, Hal file, MDE Papers, White House Series, EL; Teasley, "Ike Was Her Career," 108; Eisenhower, *Mrs. Ike,* 279.

19. Pat Nixon to Helene Drown, Feb. 3, 1953, Helene Drown Collection, Nixon Library; "DAR reception, 1953," and Jenelle M. Holland to MDE, Feb. 16, 1953, box 5, DAR—Receive file (2), White House Social Office, Tolley, EL; Lady Bird [Claudia T.] Johnson, *A White House Diary* (New York: Holt, Rinehart and Winston, 1970), 115. For group tours, also see boxes 26, 28, 29, 31, and 41 in White House Social Office, Tolley, EL.

20. West, *Upstairs at the White House,* 135; Mary Jane McCaffree Monroe, panel discussion, MDE Centennial, EL; Eisenhower, *Mrs. Ike,* 280; Anthony, *First Ladies,* 582.

21. West, *Upstairs at the White House,* 92; "Tobacco Business Is Good," *U.S. News & World Report,* Aug. 23, 1957, 44; MDE oral history, 162, EL; Brandon, *Mamie Doud Eisenhower,* 173–174.

22. Anthony, *First Ladies,* 586; Anthony, *America's First Families,* 301; Perry, *Jacqueline Kennedy,* 13.

23. MDE oral history, 163, EL; Eisenhower, *Mrs. Ike,* 280; Rose Kennedy to DDE, Nov. 11, 1954, and Jacqueline Kennedy to DDE, Nov. 1954, box 972, Sen. John F. Kennedy file, PPF, Central Files, EL; guest lists, Jan. 20, 1959, Apr. 22, Apr. 27, 1960, box 4, Heads of State Dinners file, McCaffree Papers, EL; guest lists, May 8, 1957, Oct. 17, 1957, June 17, 1958, boxes 4, 5, Scrapbooks 4, 5, White House Social Office, MDE Scrapbooks, EL; Johnson, *A White House Diary,* 699–700.

24. "Senate Ladies Picnic Luncheon," box 4, Social Functions of MDE file, McCaffree Papers, EL; Prescott Bush to MDE, May 15, 1956, and Charity Martin to MDE, May 8, 1956, box 56, Senate Ladies Luncheon file (4), White House Social Office, Tolley, EL.

25. A. B. Tolley to [Mary Jane] McCaffree, Feb. 5, 1953, box 4, Veterans Garden Parties file, McCaffree Papers, EL; guest list, garden party, May 28, 1959, box 6, Scrapbook 6, White House Social Office, MDE Scrapbooks, EL; Anthony, *First Ladies,* 580; MDE to Mrs. Wilson, May 16, 1956, box 56, Veterans Garden Party file (1), White House Social Office, Tolley, EL.

26. Mary Jane McCaffree Monroe, panel discussion, MDE Centennial, EL; Anthony, *First Ladies,* 580; Anthony, *America's First Families,* 365; "Memories of

White House Flow Back," Nov. 1966, clipping, box 1, White House file, MDE Papers, 1966 Files Series, EL.

27. West, *Upstairs at the White House,* 157; Rex Scouten, panel discussion, MDE Centennial, EL; Eisenhower, *Mandate for Change,* 262; "Children's Birthday Party List," Mar. 31, 1953, box 4, Children's Birthday Party file, White House Social Office, Tolley, EL; photo, David Eisenhower birthday party, Presidential Gallery, museum, EL.

28. "The Perfect Gift from Aunt Mamie," *Life,* Dec. 5, 1960, 42, 44; "Ellen and Mamie Moore Bow at White House Tea," *Washington Evening Star,* Nov. 26, 1960, clipping, box 6, Scrapbook 6, White House Social Office, MDE Scrapbooks, EL.

29. Mary Jane McCaffree Monroe and Mary Jean Eisenhower, panel discussion, MDE Centennial, EL; E. Frederic Morrow, *Black Man in the White House: A Diary of the Eisenhower Years by the Administrative Officer for Special Projects, The White House, 1955–1961* (New York: Coward-McCann, 1963), 112–113; Mary Evans Seeley, *Season's Greetings from the White House* (New York: MasterMedia, 1996), 70, 73; party note, Dec. 22, 1955, box 3, Scrapbook 3, party note, Dec. 22, 1958, box 5, Scrapbook 5, and party note, Dec. 22, 1960, box 6, Scrapbook 6, White House Social Office, MDE Scrapbooks, EL; MDE oral history, 164, EL.

30. Mary Jane McCaffree Monroe, MDE Centennial, EL; Senate Ladies Luncheon, Apr. 9, 1957, box 4, Social Functions of MDE file, McCaffree Papers, EL; "The Eisenhowers Revive Easter Egg Roll on Lawn," *New York Times,* Mar. 8, 1953, 20; "First Lady Revived Egg-Rolling Party," *New York Times,* Mar. 25, 1953, 29; Pollock, "How Ike Rates as a Father," 9; MDE to Perle Mesta, Apr. 9, 1953, box 29, Mrs. Perle Mesta file, MDE Papers, White House Series, EL.

31. Anthony, *First Ladies,* 580–581; Fred I. Greenstein, *The Hidden-Hand Presidency: Eisenhower as Leader* (New York: Basic Books, 1982), 5. For examples of special White House tours, see Rupert B. Clark to Mary Jane McCaffree, Jan. 28, Mar. 16, 1954, box 28; National Negro Insurance Association Agency Offices Conference file, and Irene McCoy Gaines to Valores J. Washington, Mar. 6, 1954, box 37; National Association of Colored Women file, Eleventh Regional 4-H Club Camp for Negro Boys and Girls file, and Mary Jane McCaffree to Ezra Taft Benson, June 2, 1958, box 74. All located in White House Social Office, Tolley, EL.

32. Lewis L. Gould, *The Modern American Presidency* (Lawrence: University Press of Kansas, 2003), 119; Eisenhower, *Mrs. Ike,* 301; Jack Gould, "The Case of Lucille Ball: Treatment of the Star Should Be Standard in the Industry, September 20, 1953," in *Watching Television Come of Age:* The New York Times *Reviews*

by Jack Gould, ed. Lewis L. Gould (Austin: University of Texas Press, 2002), 59–62; Desi Arnaz, *A Book* (New York: Morrow, 1976), 257.

33. Guest list, June 30, 1954, "United States Military Academy, 1915, Classmates," menu and program, and Margaret Mueller to MDE, July 4, 1954, box 36, Class of 1915—Dinner file (1), White House Social Office, Tolley, EL; David and David, *Ike and Mamie,* 209; West, *Upstairs at the White House,* 159; MDE to Grace Gruenther, Apr. 24, 1956, box 3, MDE 1956 file, E. Corres. Series, Gruenther Papers, EL.

34. "Mamie's Circle of Friends," Apr. 1, 1957, clipping, box 35, Press (1957) file, MDE Papers, White House Series, and guest list, White House lunch, June 8, 1959, box 6, Scrapbook 6, White House Social Office, MDE Scrapbooks, EL.

35. Ellis D. Slater, *The Ike I Knew* (n.p.: privately printed, 1980), 75; "Dr. Snyder's Progress Reports," July 26, Aug. 1, 1959, box 9, Medial Diary re DDE, June 1–Sept. 30, 1959 file, Snyder Papers, EL.

36. MDE to Louise Caffey, May 9, 1955, box 5, Gen. and Mrs. Benjamin Caffey file, and MDE to Kitty Smith, July 26, 1955, box 39, Gen. and Mrs. Howard Smith file, MDE Papers, White House Series, EL; MDE oral history, 164, EL.

37. Eisenhower, *Mrs. Ike,* 278; Wallace, "They Like Mamie, Too," 150; MDE to Bella Hall, box 17, Hal file, and MDE to Kitty Smith, May 6, 1953, box 39, Gen. and Mrs. Howard Smith file, MDE Papers, White House Series, EL; Slater, *The Ike I Knew,* 73.

38. West, *Upstairs at the White House,* 158; Anthony, *America's First Families,* 130; Eisenhower, *Waging Peace,* 586; Rex Scouten, panel discussion, MDE Centennial, EL.

39. Eisenhower, *Mandate for Change,* 261; Robert H. Ferrell, ed., *The Diary of James C. Hagerty: Eisenhower in Mid-Course, 1954–1955* (Bloomington: Indiana University Press, 1983), 113; MDE to Kitty Smith, July 23, 1954, box 39, MDE Papers, White House Series, EL; MDE to Grace Gruenther, Apr. 24, 1956, box 3, MDE 1956 file, E. Corres. Series, Gruenther Papers, EL; Anthony, *America's First Families,* 111; "First Family Reunion: The Grandchildren Visit 'Mimi,'" *Life,* Mar. 23, 1954, 36.

40. Eisenhower, *Mandate for Change,* 261; Eisenhower, *Mrs. Ike,* 291; Anne Eisenhower Flöttl and David Eisenhower, Eisenhower family interviews, video, Presidential Gallery, museum, EL.

41. Slater, *The Ike I Knew,* 67; Virginia Conner to MDE, ca. 1954, box 6, Con file, MDE Papers, White House Series, EL; Neal, *The Eisenhowers,* 401.

SECOND TERM AND RETIREMENT

1. Robert H. Ferrell, *Ill-Advised: Presidential Health and Public Trust* (Columbia: University of Missouri Press, 1992), 79, 84; Robert Gilbert, "Eisenhower's

Heart Attack: How It Was Handled by the White House and by the Campaign Team" (paper presented at the 1956 Presidential Election symposium, EL, Oct. 13, 2006); MDE to Louise Caffey, Sept. 28, 1955, box 5, Gen. and Mrs. Benjamin Caffey file, MDE Papers, White House Series, EL.

2. Ferrell, *Ill-Advised,* 75–78, 80, 85; Eisenhower, *Mandate for Change,* 537, 539, 540; Gilbert, "Eisenhower's Heart Attack," EL; MDE oral history, 97, EL.

3. Eisenhower, *Mandate for Change,* 543–544; guest lists, notations, box 3, Scrapbook 3, MDE Scrapbooks, White House Social Office, and Pat Nixon to MDE, Oct. 1955, box 32, Nixon file, MDE Papers, White House Series, EL.

4. "Harriman Scores Eisenhower Policy," *New York Times,* Mar. 9, 1955, 17; "G.O.P. Seen 'Right of Taft,'" *New York Times,* Mar. 10, 1955, 12; "2 Parties in Clash on Mrs. Eisenhower," *New York Times,* Mar. 11, 1955, 1, 6; "First Lady Is 'Better,'" *New York Times,* Mar. 12, 1955, 20; "Eisenhowers Entertain," *New York Times,* Mar. 13, 1955, 37; Ferrell, *Diary of James Hagerty,* 207.

5. MDE interview with Barbara Walters, Mar. 26, 1970, NBC, video, EL; Gilbert, "Eisenhower's Heart Attack," EL; Eisenhower, *Mandate for Change,* 542, 571; Robert Griffith, ed., *Ike's Letters to a Friend, 1941–1958* (Lawrence: University Press of Kansas, 1984), 161; Eisenhower, *Strictly Personal,* 183–184.

6. Brandon, *Mamie Doud Eisenhower,* 141; MDE interview with Barbara Walters, Mar. 26, 1970, NBC, video, EL; Anthony, *First Ladies,* 582.

7. Brandon, *Mamie Doud Eisenhower,* 141, 175; Susan Eisenhower, panel discussion, MDE Centennial, EL.

8. MDE to Bella Hall, Feb. 29, 1956, box 17, Hal file, MDE Papers, White House Series, EL; Furman, "Mrs. Eisenhower Retains Role of 'Good Soldier' for General," *New York Times,* Mar. 1, 1956, 15.

9. Anthony, *First Ladies,* 574; Eisenhower, *Mrs. Ike,* 295; "First Lady Busy at Walter Reed," June 22, 1956, clipping, box 35, Press (1955–1956) file, MDE Papers, White House Series, EL; MDE to Grace and Al Gruenther, June 11, 1956, box 3, MDE 1956 file, E. Corres. Series, Gruenther Papers, EL.

10. Michael Birkner, "They Liked Ike, Period: The Status Quo Election of 1956" (paper presented at 1956 Presidential Election symposium, EL, Oct. 13, 2006); "Ike's Health and Politics," *Newsweek,* Aug. 20, 1956, 32; Will Stevens, "12,000 Jam Union Square as Ike and Mamie Arrive for Big Event," *San Francisco Examiner,* Aug. 22, 1956, 1, box 3, Collection of Family Memorabilia and Newspapers re Dwight D. Eisenhower, Elivera M. Doud Papers, EL.

11. "George Did It," *Newsweek,* Sept. 3, 1956, 29.

12. Griffith, *Ike's Letters to a Friend,* 171; "Women Near End of Busy Campaign," *New York Times,* Nov. 4, 1956, 69; "1956 Election," typescript, pp. 15–16, box 5, Campaign Information for Memoir file, McCaffree Papers, EL.

13. Allen, *Eisenhower and the Mass Media,* 89–93; Gilbert, "Eisenhower's Heart Attack," EL; J. Ronald Oakley, *God's Country: America in the Fifties* (New York: Dembner Books, 1986), 108–109.

14. Exhibit script, Presidential Gallery, museum, EL; Anthony, *America's First Families,* 248; West, *Upstairs at the White House,* 158–159.

15. Anthony, *First Ladies,* 575; Allen, *Eisenhower and the Mass Media,* 141–143, 207; Paul Vathis, "At 73, Mamie Treasures Half a Century of Life with Ike," *Wichita (KS) Eagle,* Nov. 14, 1969, 13A; "Women Near End of Busy Campaign," 69.

16. Allen, *Eisenhower and the Mass Media,* 108–109, 143; "Mrs. Eisenhower Is Serenaded," *New York Times,* Mar. 23, 1956, 17; Eisenhower, *Waging Peace,* 55.

17. Eisenhower, *Strictly Personal,* 188.

18. Anthony, *America's First Families,* 113. For letters to Ike and newspaper clippings, see box 551, Eisenhower Children and School Integration Problem file, PPF, Central Files, EL.

19. "General Snyder's Progress Reports," Sept. 16 and Oct. 2, 1958, box 8, Medical Diary re DDE file (3), Snyder Papers, EL; Clarence G. Lasby, *Eisenhower's Heart Attack: How Ike Beat Heart Disease and Held on to the Presidency* (Lawrence: University Press of Kansas, 1997), 270; Ferrell, *Ill-Advised,* 142–143; Eisenhower, *Waging Peace,* 228; "Why Mamie Stays Home," *Newsweek,* Feb. 8, 1960, 31; Conner, *What Father Forbad,* 120–121; Anthony, *First Ladies,* 587.

20. Eisenhower, *Waging Peace,* 6; DDE to Pat Nixon, Mar. 14, 1960, box 959, Richard Nixon file, PPF, Central Files, EL; Eisenhower, *Pat Nixon,* 194–195; Eisenhower, *Mrs. Ike,* 300; Milton Eisenhower, *The President Is Calling* (Garden City, NY: Doubleday, 1974), 325, 334.

21. Ferrell, *Ill-Advised,* 42; "General Snyder's Progress Report," Feb, 11, 1958, box 8, Medical Diary re DDE, Jan. 1–June 30, 1958 file (2), Snyder Papers, EL.

22. West, *Upstairs at the White House,* 136, 239; MDE interview with Vivian Cadden, typescript, p. 7, box 2, Ca file (1), MDE Papers, 1966 Files Series, EL; Anthony, *America's First Families,* 196; David and David, *Ike and Mamie,* 210; *White House Staff Book, 1953–61* (Washington, DC: privately printed, 1961), 6; "Soldier and Bride: 1959 and 1916," *New York Times,* July 2, 1959, 10; MDE interview with Barbara Walters, ABC, *20/20,* Nov. 1, 1979, video, EL.

23. MDE to Geneva Davis, Aug. 31, 1953, box 10, Davi file, MDE Papers, White House Series, EL; MDE to Mary Newton, May 16, 1966, and Mary Newton

to MDE, Aug. 1966, box 9, N file (3), MDE Papers, 1966 Files Series, EL; Teasley, "Ike Was Her Career," 109. Mary Newton correspondence also is located in box 32, Mrs. Mary Newton file, MDE Papers, White House Series, EL.

24. MDE to Al Gruenther, Oct. 16, 1952, box 3, MDE file (2), E. Corres. Series, Gruenther Papers, EL; Brandon, *Mamie Doud Eisenhower,* 296, 303; Stuart Symington to MDE, Feb. 20, 1953, box 33, Su file (2), MDE Papers, White House Series, EL; Carl Anthony, panel discussion, MDE Centennial, EL.

25. "Kinds of Letters, 1953," box 35, Press Requests file (1), and MDE to Pat Nixon, Nov. 16, 1954, and MDE to Patricia Nixon and MDE to Julie Nixon, Nov. 17, 1954, and MDE to Pat Nixon, Nov. 15, 1957, box 32, Nixon file, MDE Papers, White House Series, EL.

26. MDE to Grace Gruenther, May 21, 1954, box 3, MDE 1954 file, E. Corres. Series, Gruenther Papers, EL; Seeley, *Season's Greetings from the White House,* 70, 74, 75, 81, 84; Christmas card collection, archives and museum exhibits, EL.

27. Eisenhower, *Strictly Personal,* 182; Pat Nixon to MDE, Oct. 1955, and MDE to Pat Nixon, Oct. 18, 1955, box 32, Nixon file, MDE Papers, White House Series, EL.

28. Teasley, "Ike Was Her Career," 109; Annie Mae Haeman to MDE, Oct. 6, 1963, box 3, H file (1), MDE Papers, 1963 Files Series, EL. For examples of People to People advice, see MDE to Peggy Cottle, Mar. 28, 1963, and MDE to Sue Frazier, Apr. 17, 1963, box 1, School Notes, Misc. file, MDE Papers, 1963 Files Series, EL.

29. MDE to Kathy and Sally West, Mar. 25, 1954, box 45, Wes file (1), and MDE to Pat Nixon, Aug. 20, 1954, box 32, Pat and Dick Nixon file, MDE Papers, White House Series, EL; Harry F. Rosenthal, "Former First Ladies Continue Lives," *Kansas City Star,* Mar. 20, 1977, 9C.

30. "Kinds of Letters," 1953, box 35, Press Requests file (1), MDE Papers, White House Series, EL. For requests, responses, and thank-you letters, see box 9, Contributions file, MDE Papers, White House Series, EL.

31. West, *Upstairs at the White House,* 157; Anthony, *America's First Families,* 179; Alice M. Haggerty, Christ Child Farm for Convalescent Children, to MDE, Dec. 22, 1954, Clyde E. Murray, Manhattanville Community Center, to MDE, Dec. 20, 1954, and "To Receive Television Set" list of recipients, ca. 1954, box 6, Charities file, MDE Papers, White House Series, EL.

32. Anthony, *First Ladies,* 586; Eisenhower, *Mrs. Ike,* 279; exhibit script, Mamie Gallery, museum, EL; Roberts, *Rating the First Ladies,* 271–272. For charities and organizations, see boxes 1 and 2, Scrapbooks 1 and 2, White House Social Office, MDE Scrapbooks, EL.

33. Caroli, *First Ladies*, 240; Public Service Announcements, Federal Civil Defense announcement, May 1953, and American Red Cross announcement, Mar. 21, 1953, box 42, Statements (Public Service) file, MDE Papers, White House Series, EL; May, *Homeward Bound*, 93; Ferrell, *Diary of James Hagerty*, 63.

34. Truman, *First Ladies*, 215; West, *Upstairs at the White House*, 194; Rex Scouten, panel discussion, MDE Centennial, EL.

35. Margaret Brown Klapthor, *Official White House China, 1789 to the Present* (Washington, DC: Smithsonian Institution Press, 1975), 7, 13; Betty C. Monkman, *The White House: Its Historic Furnishings and First Families* (New York: Abbeville Press, 2000), 224; Aikman, "Inside the White House," 37; Mary Jane McCaffree Monroe and Rex Scouten, panel discussion, MDE Centennial, EL.

36. Eisenhower, *Pat Nixon*, 264–265; Julie Nixon Eisenhower to author, Aug. 15, 2006.

37. Caroli, *First Ladies*, 251–252; Anthony, *First Ladies*, 586–587.

38. Ripley, "'A Part of History': An Intimate Message from Washington," clipping, box 3, MDE 1961–1962 file, E. Corres. Series, Gruenther Papers, EL; "The Perfect Gift from Aunt Mamie," *Life*, Dec. 5, 1960, 44.

39. Eisenhower, *Waging Peace*, 618; "A Rare Picture Visit: The First Lady at Home," *Life*, Oct. 20, 1958, 32; MDE to Bella Hall, July 9, 1957, box 17, Hal file, MDE Papers, White House Series, EL; Eisenhower, *Mrs. Ike*, 305.

40. "Bob Hope to Help Dedicate Mamie Eisenhower's Birthplace," *Topeka (KS) Capital-Journal*, June 22, 1980, 19; Eisenhower, *Mrs. Ike*, 307; Donovan, *Confidential Secretary*, 161; DDE to Ann Whitman, Apr. 11, 1967, box 1, Correspondence, DDE file (1), Whitman Papers, EL; Neal, *The Eisenhowers*, 461–462; James Edward Schaaf, *Mamie Doud Eisenhower and Her Chicken Farmer Cousin* (n.p.: privately printed, 1974), 62–69; "Mamie" video, Mamie Gallery, museum, EL. For a brief history of Eisenhower College, see David L. Dresser, *Eisenhower College: The Life and Death of a Living Memorial* (Interlaken, NY: Heart of the Lakes Publishing, 1995).

41. Kirk, *Music in the White House*, 276; Eisenhower, *Mrs. Ike*, 307; Perry, *Jacqueline Kennedy*, 145; Lillian "Rusty" Brown to Robert Montgomery, memo, Nov. 4, 1963, box 5, National Cultural Center file, MDE Papers, 1963 Series, EL.

42. Eisenhower, *Mrs. Ike*, 310.

43. Ibid., 311, 314; MDE to Howard Young, Jan. 13, 1969, box 1, Correspondence—Letters from MDE file, Young Papers, EL; MDE interview with Vivian Cadden, typescript, p. 7, box 2, Ca file, MDE Papers, 1966 Files Series, EL.

44. Eisenhower, *The President Is Calling,* 334; Eisenhower, *Mrs. Ike,* 314; Eisenhower, *Special People,* 189–191; MDE to Ann Whitman, Apr. 28, 1969, box 1, Correspondence—E file, Whitman Papers, EL; MDE oral history, 109, EL.

45. Eisenhower, *Mrs. Ike,* 316, 317; MDE to Howard Young, Apr. 29, 1969, box 1, Correspondence—Letters to MDE file, Young Papers, EL; MDE to Grace and Al Gruenther, Oct. 13, 1972, box 4, MDE 1971–1973 file, E. Corres. Series, Gruenther Papers, EL.

46. David Halberstam, *The Fifties* (New York: Villard Books, 1993), 328; Eisenhower, *Pat Nixon,* 161–162, 278; MDE interview with Barbara Walters, ABC *20/20,* Nov. 1979, video, EL; Barbara Eisenhower Foltz, interview with author; Pat Nixon to Helene Drown, Feb. 3, 1953, Helene Drown Collection, Nixon Library; "Dinner at the White House, Jan. 19, 1954," guest list, box 24, Vice-President Nixon Dinner file (1), White House Social Office, Tolley, EL; Slater, *The Ike I Knew,* 66–67.

47. Anthony, *First Ladies,* 583; Eisenhower, *Waging Peace,* 486; appointment book, May 17, 1955, and diary entry, Jan. 9, 1958, Pat Nixon Papers, Nixon Library; Eisenhower, *Pat Nixon,* 164, 422.

48. George Gallup, "Mamie Eisenhower, U.S. Grande Dame," *Kansas City Star,* Dec. 27, 1970, 18A; Harry F. Rosenthal, "Former First Ladies Continue Lives," *Kansas City Star,* Mar. 20, 1977, 1C.

49. Eisenhower, *Mrs. Ike,* 330, 332.

50. Marian Christy, *Boston Globe,* Nov. 5, 1979, cited in "Mamie" video, Presidential Gallery, museum, EL.

BIBLIOGRAPHIC ESSAY

The primary documents pertaining to Mamie Doud Eisenhower are in the collections of the Eisenhower Presidential Library, Abilene, Kansas. The library's holdings include personal letters, public mail, official correspondence, press statements, scrapbooks, and documentation that encompass the duties of a first lady. Documents from the prepresidential years are held in the Barbara Thompson Eisenhower Papers. This collection, rich with Mamie Eisenhower's personal correspondence to friends and to her parents, was donated to the library by Mamie's daughter-in-law. It is an important resource for the prepresidential years that includes the Eisenhowers' experiences in post–World War I Paris, in Panama, in Washington during the 1930s, and in the Philippines, and Mamie's life in Washington during World War II. The collection of Mamie Eisenhower documents for after World War II is separated into the Columbia Series, covering the time in which the Eisenhowers were at Columbia University (1948–1950); the SHAPE Series (1951–1952), for the period when the Eisenhowers were in Paris during Ike's service as head of Supreme Headquarters, Allied Powers Europe; and the White House Series, the most important collection for Mamie's role as first lady. The materials in this series include private and public correspondence, files related to her duties as White House hostess, interests and work with charitable organizations, public service announcements, and her relations with the press. Two additional series cover the postpresidential years, the 1963 Files Series and the 1966 Files Series. These files contain correspondence, as well as documents related to charitable projects and organizations.

In addition to the papers of Mamie Doud Eisenhower, the library holds the transcript of an oral history interview conducted with Mrs. Eisenhower in 1972 by Dr. Maclyn Burg and Dr. John Wickman; videos of Barbara Walters's television interviews with Mrs. Eisenhower conducted in 1970 and 1979; videos of presentations and panel discussions during the Mamie Doud Eisenhower Centennial held at the library in November 1996; and videos of interviews with family members and relevant film clips that are shown in the Mamie Gallery and Presidential Gallery in the presidential library's museum. Exhibits in the museum's Mamie Gallery and Presidential Gallery, as well as the helpful information provided by curator Dennis Medina, who knew Mrs. Eisenhower and worked with her on the collections, added another layer of information to printed and video documentation.

Other collections at the Eisenhower Library contributed additional perspective and information related to Mamie Eisenhower. First, there is the collection of Mrs. Eisenhower's personal secretary, Mary Jane McCaffree (Monroe); these are separated into White House social events, the postpresidential years, and a "miscellaneous" file that includes material for the 1952 campaign. Social engagements, guest lists, event notes, and memos among the East Wing staff are contained in the A. B. Tolley files of the White House Social Office. Also consulted for this volume were the George B. Bookman Papers, 1981–1993, whose typescript of Gabriel Hauge's biography is relevant to the 1952 campaign. Other useful collections were the Jacqueline Cochran Papers, 1932–1975 (she and her husband were personal friends and staunch Ike supporters); Elivera M. Doud Papers (Mamie's mother and a frequent resident in the White House); Alfred M. Gruenther Papers, 1941–1983 (the Gruenthers were personal friends, and General Gruenther followed Ike at NATO); Howard Young Papers, 1946–1970 (a New York art dealer and personal friend who lent his Wisconsin cabin to the Eisenhowers for vacations); and Ann C. Whitman Personal Papers (Ike's White House secretary). For information regarding both Mamie's and Ike's medical history there are the Wallace Sullivan Papers, the Col. [Dr.] Thomas W. Mattingly Papers, and the Dr. Howard McCrum Snyder Papers.

Also of interest are the papers and panel discussion from the October 13, 2006, Eisenhower Library symposium, "The 1956 Presidential Election: Was It a Foregone Conclusion?" The library also holds the oral history interviews of Barbara Thompson Eisenhower Foltz, Mamie's daughter-in-law, and those of John and Delores Moaney, who were employed by the Eisenhowers at Fort Myer, through the White House years, and at Gettysburg. Unfortunately, these interviews are still closed to researchers, but Mrs. Foltz did agree to answer a number of questions submitted by the author.

Few biographies have been written on Mamie Eisenhower. Dorothy Brandon's *Mamie Doud Eisenhower: A Portrait of a First Lady* (New York: Scribner's, 1954) is limited in its usefulness for the entire presidential period, but all the same, Brandon had access to Mrs. Eisenhower, who seemed to realize that Brandon's work introduced the first lady to the American people. Brandon's biography offers insights to the first lady that were not available until Susan Eisenhower's *Mrs. Ike: Memories and Reflections on the Life of Mamie Eisenhower* (New York: Farrar, Straus and Giroux, 1996). In that volume, the first lady's granddaughter blends personal reminiscences with biography. Personal yet objective, the volume provides readers with a feeling of firsthand access to Mamie, and it provides family stories and viewpoints that otherwise would not be available. Personal memoir also mixes with biography in Julie Nixon Eisenhower's chapter on Mamie in *Special People* (New York: Simon and Schuster, 1977), which largely focuses on how Mrs. Eisenhower faced her husband's last heart attack and death. Of the other biographies, Alden Hatch's *Red Carpet for Mamie* (New York: Holt, Rinehart and Winston, 1954) must be taken with a dose of caution, despite the fact that Hatch had credentials as a professional biographer; D. L. Kimball's *I Remember Mamie* (Fayette, IA: Trends and Events, 1981) is based on secondary sources, some available at the Mamie Doud Eisenhower Birthplace in Boone, Iowa; and James Schaaf's *Mamie Doud Eisenhower and Her Chicken Farmer Cousin* (n.p.: privately printed, 1974) offers family-related stories that are often peripheral to the subject of the first lady. Finally, there is Lester David and Irene David, *Ike and Mamie: The Story of the General and His Lady* (New York: Putnam's, 1981). Journalistic in tone, this volume provides general biographical information, but it contains factual errors and has a tendency to generalize the Eisenhowers as one-dimensional characters. Although Steve Neal's *The Eisenhowers: Reluctant Dynasty* (Garden City, NY: Doubleday, 1978) is not devoted to Mamie, and its information for her is based primarily on secondary sources, it is worth a look. Particularly good articles on Mrs. Eisenhower were Lonnelle Aikman, "Inside the White House," *National Geographic,* Jan. 1961, 3–43; Martin M. Teasley, "Ike Was Her Career,"

Prologue 19 (Summer 1987): 107–115; Robert Wallace, "They Like Mamie, Too," *Life*, Oct. 13, 1952, 149–150. Additional articles from *Time, Life, U.S. News & World Report, Newsweek,* the *New York Times,* and other newspapers are cited in the text.

Volumes written or edited by members of the Eisenhower family were helpful in fleshing out events and providing firsthand accounts from those who were close to the first lady. These are important for a more comprehensive view of Mamie Eisenhower's personal life and her close relationships with family. John S. D. Eisenhower's edited volume, *Letters to Mamie: Dwight D. Eisenhower* (Garden City, NY: Doubleday, 1978), contains the letters Ike wrote to Mamie during World War II. Although her letters are not extant, one often gains a sense of what she wrote to her husband from his replies. John S. D. Eisenhower's *Strictly Personal* (Garden City, NY: Doubleday, 1974) is autobiographical, and understandably includes stories that relate to his parents, life in the White House, and Ike's health problems. Ike's writings also add to the picture of Mamie's place in events and their personal relationship. The volumes consulted were Dwight D. Eisenhower, *At Ease: Stories I Tell to Friends* (Garden City, NY: Doubleday, 1967); *The White House Years: Mandate for Change, 1953–1956* (Garden City, NY: Doubleday, 1963); and *The White House Years: Waging Peace, 1956–1961* (Garden City, NY: Doubleday, 1965). Additionally, *Eisenhower: The Prewar Diaries and Selected Papers, 1905–1941,* edited by Daniel D. Holt and James W. Leyerzapf and published by Johns Hopkins University Press in 1998, was especially helpful for the prewar years.

Certainly not all of the many volumes or articles devoted to Dwight D. Eisenhower would have been useful for this study, but a number added context, as well as informative references to Mamie Eisenhower. These included Stephen E. Ambrose's *Eisenhower: Soldier, General of the Army, President-Elect, 1890–1952,* vol. 1 (New York: Simon and Schuster, 1983), as well as his *Eisenhower: The President* (New York: Simon and Schuster, 1984) and "The Eisenhower Presidency: An Assessment," in *The Eisenhower Presidency and the 1950s,* ed. Michael S. Mayer (New York: Houghton Mifflin, 1998). Other publications related to Eisenhower consulted for this volume were Carlo D'Este, *Eisenhower: A Soldier's Story* (New York: Holt, 2002); Milton S. Eisenhower, *The President Is Calling* (Garden City,

NY: Doubleday, 1974); John L. Helgerson, *Getting to Know the President: CIA Briefings of Presidential Candidates, 1952–1992* (Washington, DC: Center for the Study of Intelligence, Central Intelligence Agency, ca. 1994); Travis Beal Jacobs, *Eisenhower at Columbia* (New Brunswick, NJ: Transaction, 2001); Clarence G. Lasby, *Eisenhower's Heart Attack: How Ike Beat Heart Disease and Held on to the Presidency* (Lawrence: University Press of Kansas, 1997); Robert H. Ferrell, *Ill-Advised: Presidential Health and Public Trust* (Columbia: University of Missouri Press, 1992); Fred I. Greenstein, *The Hidden-Hand Presidency: Eisenhower as Leader* (New York: Basic Books, 1982); Ellis D. Slater, *The Ike I Knew* (n.p.: privately printed, 1980); and Brigadier General Arthur S. Nevins, *Gettysburg's Five-Star Farmer* (New York: Carlton Press, 1977). Also consulted were Michael R. Beschloss, *Eisenhower: A Centennial Life* (New York: HarperCollins, 1990); Robert H. Ferrell, ed., *The Eisenhower Diaries* (New York: Norton, 1981); Lewis L. Gould, *The Modern American Presidency* (Lawrence: University Press of Kansas, 2003); Chester J. Pach Jr. and Elmo Richardson, *The Presidency of Dwight D. Eisenhower* (Lawrence: University Press of Kansas, 1991); and Daniel D. Holt, "An Unlikely Partnership and Service: Dwight D. Eisenhower, Mark Clark, and the Philippines," *Kansas History* 13 (Autumn 1990): 149–165. Material related specifically to the subjects of school integration and the Eisenhower grandchildren, as well as President Eisenhower's letters to Pat and Richard Nixon and letters written to Eisenhower by Rose and Jacqueline Kennedy were located in the President's Personal File, Central Files, at the Eisenhower Library.

Also helpful were publications that focused on individuals who worked within the Eisenhower administration. Ike's press secretary James Hagerty is represented by Robert H. Ferrell, ed., *The Diary of James C. Hagerty: Eisenhower in Mid-Course, 1954–1955* (Bloomington: Indiana University Press, 1983), while Ike's personal secretary is featured in Robert J. Donovan, *Confidential Secretary: Ann Whitman's 20 Years with Eisenhower and Rockefeller* (New York: Dutton, 1988). E. Frederic Morrow's *Black Man in the White House: A Diary of the Eisenhower Years by the Administrative Officer for Special Projects, The White House, 1955–1961* (New York: Coward-McCann, 1963) is cited in the text for its few references to Mamie, but it is useful for one viewpoint on the administration's handling of civil rights issues. Another insider's view is J. B. West, *Upstairs at the White House: My Life with the First Ladies* (New York: Coward, McCann and Geoghegan, 1973); West moved from usher to head usher during the Eisenhower years, and thus had almost daily contact with the first lady. Not directly relevant to the Eisenhower years, but useful for references to those within the administration, was Walter Trohan's *Political Animals: Memoirs of a Sentimental Cynic* (Garden City, NY: Doubleday, 1975).

Several of the publications already cited dealt in one way or another with the lingering story of Kay Summersby. In addressing the subject for this study, Summersby's own writings were consulted. These included "Kay's War," *Time*, Sept. 27, 1948, 26; Kay Summersby, *Eisenhower Was My Boss* (New York: Prentice-Hall, 1948); and Kay Summersby Morgan, *Past Forgetting: My Love Affair with Dwight D. Eisenhower* (New York: Simon and Schuster, 1975). For the latter book, Summersby worked with ghostwriter Barbara Wyden, whose papers are at the Eisenhower Presidential Library.

Although this study was not designed as a comparative history, the differences or similarities between Mamie Eisenhower and other modern first ladies had to be addressed at particular junctures. Important, too, were Mrs. Eisenhower's personal relationships with these first ladies. Most useful in this avenue of investigation were Julie Nixon Eisenhower, *Pat Nixon: The Untold Story* (New York: Simon and Schuster, 1986); Lady Bird [Claudia T.] Johnson, *A White House Diary* (New York: Holt, Rinehart and Winston, 1970); Joseph P. Lash, *A World of Love: Eleanor Roosevelt and Her Friends, 1943–1962* (Garden City, NY: Doubleday, 1984); Barbara A. Perry, *Jacqueline Kennedy: First Lady of the New Frontier* (Lawrence: University Press of Kansas, 2004); Steve Neal, ed., *Eleanor and Harry: The Correspondence of Eleanor Roosevelt and Harry S. Truman* (New York: Scribner's, 2002); Eleanor Roosevelt, *This I Remember* (New York: Harper and Brothers, 1949); and Nancy Beck Young, *Lou Henry Hoover: Activist First Lady* (Lawrence: University Press of Kansas, 2004). Not cited in the text but of interest for Eleanor Roosevelt's handling of White House correspondence is Robert Cohen's *Dear Mrs. Roosevelt: Letters from Children of the Great Depression* (Chapel Hill: University of North Carolina Press, 2002). Cohen notes that Mrs. Roosevelt believed that she revamped the ponderous bureaucratic responses that went out to those who wrote to her, but in fact little changed from the standard form letters for the majority of responses.

In the past few years, a number of book publications and articles have dealt with the subjects of first ladies and first families. Obviously, some are more thoughtful and offer more than others. To my mind the most comprehensive and enlightening are Carl Sferrazza Anthony's *First Ladies: The Saga of the Presidents' Wives and Their Power, 1789–1961* (New York: Quill/William Morrow, 1990), and his *America's First Families: An Inside View of 200 Years of Private Life in the White House* (New York: Touchstone, Simon and Schuster, 2000). Also consulted and cited in the text are Betty Boyd Caroli, *First Ladies*, 2nd ed. (Garden City, NY: Doubleday Direct, 1997); Gil Troy, *Mrs. and Mrs. President: From the Trumans to the Clintons*, 2nd rev. ed. (Lawrence: University Press of Kansas, 2000); Lewis L. Gould, "Modern First Ladies: An Institutional Perspective," *Prologue* 19 (Summer 1987): 71–83, and his *American First Ladies: Their Lives and Their Legacy* (New York: Routledge, 2001). There is also Margaret Truman's *First Ladies* (New York: Random House, 1995), and rather limited in content, but nonetheless of interest, is John B. Roberts II, *Rating the First Ladies: The Women Who Influenced the Presidency* (New York: Kensington, 2003). Myra Gutin's *The President's Partner: The First Lady in the Twentieth Century* (Greenwood, CT: Greenwood Press, 1989), on the other hand, offers nothing of consequence on Mamie Eisenhower and on some points is factually inaccurate. Not cited in the text are Paul F. Boller Jr., *Presidential Wives* (New York: Oxford University Press, 1998) and Edith P. Mayo and Denise D. Meringolo, *First Ladies: Political Role and Public Image* (Washington, DC: National Museum of American History, 1994).

To better understand Mamie Eisenhower's personal imprint on the White House, the following volumes were particularly helpful: Elise K. Kirk, *Music at the White House: A History of the American Spirit* (Urbana: University of Illinois Press, 1986); Betty C. Monkman, *The White House: Its Historic Furnishings and First Families* (New York: Abbeville Press, 2000); Mary Evans Seeley, *Season's Greetings from the White House* (New York: MasterMedia, 1996); and Margaret Brown Klapthor, *Official White House China, 1789 to the Present* (Washington, DC: Smithsonian Institution Press, 1975), in which Mrs. Eisenhower provided the introduction. Mrs. Eisenhower also wrote the introduction for a reprint of Lydia Spencer Lane's *I Married a Soldier, or Old Days in the Old Army* (Philadelphia: Lippincott, 1893; reprint, Albuquerque, NM: Horn and Wallace, 1964). The first lady did not, however, write her own reminiscences of army life. Nor did most of the women of her generation, unlike their nineteenth-century counterparts. The two notable exceptions among Mamie's acquaintances were two autobiographies: Maurine Clark, *Captain's Bride, General's Lady: The Memoir of Mrs. Mark W. Clark* (New York: McGraw-Hill, 1956), and Virginia Conner, *What Father Forbad* (Philadelphia: Dorrance, 1951).

Mamie Eisenhower was involved in two successful presidential campaigns. In midcentury America these bridged the old-fashioned tradition of whistle-stops by train to the new age of television campaigning. Changes in campaign methods were addressed by Bernard Benjamin Yamron's "From Whistle Stops to Polispots: Political Advertising and Presidential Politics in the United States, 1948–1980" (Ph.D. diss., Brown University, 1995). Mamie's press relations, as well as the use of television in campaigning, are discussed in Craig Allen's *Eisenhower and the Mass Media: Peace, Prosperity, and Prime-Time TV* (Chapel Hill: University of North Carolina Press, 1993). That publication is far more enlightening in terms of the role of the media and its relationship with the first lady than Maurine H. Beasley's *First Ladies and the Press: The Unfinished Partnership of the Media Age* (Evanston, IL: Northwestern University Press, 2005), which is rather disappointing in its lack of insightful discussion or exploration of Mamie Eisenhower. Also consulted for references to negative press, specifically that which appeared in the columns of Drew Pearson, was Tyler Abell, ed., *Drew Pearson Diaries, 1949–1959* (New York: Holt, Rinehart and Winston, 1974).

It was necessary to discuss Mamie Eisenhower within the context of her times. She came of age when the New Woman/Outdoor Girl of the early twentieth century emerged as a counterpoint to the Victorian woman. Informative volumes for this cultural change were Beth L. Bailey's excellent *From Front Porch to Back Seat: Courtship in Twentieth-Century America* (Baltimore: Johns Hopkins University Press, 1989); Maureen Honey, ed., *Breaking the Ties That Bind: Popular Stories of the New Woman, 1915–1930* (Norman: University of

Oklahoma Press, 1992); Rosalind Rosenberg, *Separate Spheres: Intellectual Roots of Modern Feminism* (New Haven, CT: Yale University Press, 1982); and Lois Rudnick, "The New Woman," in *1915, The Cultural Moment,* ed. Adele Heller and Lois Rudnick (New Brunswick, NJ: Rutgers University Press, 1991).

The cultural context of the 1950s was an essential element, and one that demanded a look at several issues. These included the popular culture, women as housewives and as wage earners, the atomic age and the cold war, the family and the baby boom. As Stephanie Coontz points out in *The Way We Never Were: American Families and the Nostalgia Trap* (New York: Basic Books, 1992), nostalgia for the decade has overshadowed its realities. One of those realities was the cold war and the threat of nuclear attack. Elaine Tyler May's *Homeward Bound: American Families in the Cold War Era,* rev. ed. (New York: Basic Books, 1999) considers how that threat was expressed within the nuclear family, as does her "Cold War—Warm Hearth," in *The Eisenhower Presidency and the 1950s,* ed. Michael S. Mayer (New York: Houghton Mifflin, 1998). Steven Mintz and Susan Kellogg also considered the family in *Domestic Revolutions: A Social History of American Family Life* (New York: Free Press, 1988), while the complexities of women's roles were discussed in William H. Chafe's *The Paradox of Change: American Women in the 20th Century* (New York: Oxford University Press, 1991) and in Joanne Meyerowitz's edited volume *Not June Cleaver: Women and Gender in Postwar America, 1945–1960* (Philadelphia: Temple University Press, 1994). Not cited in the text but informative for changing marriage patterns was Nancy F. Cott, *Public Vows: A History of Marriage and the Nation* (Cambridge MA: Harvard University Press, 2000).

For statistical reports on women in the workforce during the 1950s, the following were useful: Robert W. Smuts, *Women and Work in America* (New York: Columbia University Press, 1959), and National Manpower Council, *Womanpower: A Statement by the National Manpower Council* (New York: Columbia University Press, 1957). The changes brought by technology clearly had an impact on the work of women in the home and on women as consumers. Not cited in the text but useful for general discussions for the changing face of domesticity were Ruth Schwartz Cowan's *More Work for Mother: The Ironies of Household Technology from the Open Hearth to the Microwave* (New York: Basic Books, 1983), and Glenna Matthews's *"Just a Housewife": The Rise and Fall of Domesticity in America* (New York: Oxford University Press, 1987).

Numerous publications have touched on some aspect of the popular culture of the 1950s. Among those consulted for this study were Brian S. Alexander, *Atomic Kitchen: Gadgets and Inventions for Yesterday's Cook* (Portland, OR: Collectors Press, 2004); Lewis Gould, ed., *Watching Television Come of Age:* The New York Times *Reviews by Jack Gould* (Austin: University of Texas Press, 2002); David Halberstam, *The Fifties* (New York: Villard Books, 1993); Karal Ann Marling, *As Seen on TV: The Visual Culture of Everyday Life in the 1950s* (Cambridge, MA: Harvard University Press, 1994); and Lary May, ed., *Recasting America: Culture and Politics in the Age of Cold War* (Chicago: University of Chicago Press, 1989). Of particular use in the latter volume was Clifford E. Clark Jr., "Ranch-House Suburbia: Ideals and Realities." Two other volumes dealing with the era, in terms of the relationship between cultural changes, television, religion, and the influence of cold war politics, are J. Ronald Oakley, *God's Country: America in the Fifties* (New York: Dembner Books, 1986), and Stephen J. Whitfield, *The Culture of the Cold War* (Baltimore: Johns Hopkins University Press, 1991).

INDEX